Learn SwiftUI

An introductory guide to creating intuitive cross-platform user interfaces using Swift 5

Chris Barker

BIRMINGHAM - MUMBAI

Learn SwiftUI

Commissioning Editor: Pavan Ramchandani
Acquisition Editor: Heramb Bhavsar
Content Development Editor: Akhil Nair
Senior Editor: Hayden Edwards
Technical Editor: Jane DSouza
Copy Editor: Safis Editing
Project Coordinator: Kinjal Bari
Proofreader: Safis Editing
Indexer: Priyanka Dhadke
Production Designer: Nilesh Mohite

First published: April 2020

Production reference: 1020420

Published by Packt Publishing Ltd.
Livery Place
35 Livery Street
Birmingham
B3 2PB, UK.

ISBN 978-1-83921-542-1

www.packt.com

For my partner Mandy, who is the strongest and bravest woman I have ever met, and to our beautiful daughter Madeleine. Thank you both for your love and support.

For Dudley...

– Chris Barker

Subscribe to our online digital library for full access to over 7,000 books and videos, as well as industry leading tools to help you plan your personal development and advance your career. For more information, please visit our website.

Why subscribe?

- Spend less time learning and more time coding with practical eBooks and Videos from over 4,000 industry professionals

- Improve your learning with Skill Plans built especially for you

- Get a free eBook or video every month

- Fully searchable for easy access to vital information

- Copy and paste, print, and bookmark content

Did you know that Packt offers eBook versions of every book published, with PDF and ePub files available? You can upgrade to the eBook version at www.packt.com and as a print book customer, you are entitled to a discount on the eBook copy. Get in touch with us at customercare@packtpub.com for more details.

At www.packt.com, you can also read a collection of free technical articles, sign up for a range of free newsletters, and receive exclusive discounts and offers on Packt books and eBooks.

Contributors

About the author

Chris Barker is a senior iOS developer and tech lead for fashion retailer N Brown (JD Williams, SimplyBe, Jacamo), where he heads the iOS team, building apps for their major brands. Having now worked in the IT industry for over 22 years, Chris started his career developing .NET applications for online retailer dabs.com (now BT Shop).

In 2014, he made his move into mobile app development with digital agency Openshadow based in MediaCityUK. Here, he worked on mobile apps for clients such as Louis Vuitton and L'Oréal Paris. Chris often attends and speaks at his local iOS developer meetup, NSManchester.

Most recently, Chris attended Malaga Mobile in Spain, where he spoke about his passion for accessibility in mobile apps. Over the past 2 years, Chris has been a regular speaker at CodeMobile Developer Conference and plans to return in the future.

To everyone who has inspired and supported me during my career not only as a developer but as a first-time author too. From my first mentor, Kerry, who took me under her wing to my current apprentices, who keep me on my toes daily – thank you. A shout out to my technical reviewer, Juan, who was a light at the end of the tunnel after many months of self-doubt – thank you. To the entire team at Packt for their patience, guidance, and understanding during this whole process – thank you.

About the reviewer

Juan Catalan is a software developer with more than 10 years of experience, having started learning iOS almost from the beginning. He has worked as a professional iOS developer in many industries, including industrial automation, transportation, document management, fleet tracking, real estate, and financial services. Juan has contributed to more than 30 published apps, some of them with millions of users. He has a passion for software architecture, always looking for ways to write better code and optimize a mobile app.

Packt is searching for authors like you

If you're interested in becoming an author for Packt, please visit `authors.packtpub.com` and apply today. We have worked with thousands of developers and tech professionals, just like you, to help them share their insight with the global tech community. You can make a general application, apply for a specific hot topic that we are recruiting an author for, or submit your own idea.

Table of Contents

Preface

SwiftUI is the brand new UI framework unveiled by Apple at WWDC 2019. For iOS, it comes as a potential successor to UIKit and AppKit for macOS.

SwiftUI takes full advantage of declarative syntax, changing the way we think about designing and developing apps.

We start by taking a look at the Swift programming language before moving onto how declarative syntax works so well for SwiftUI. We'll then begin to program our very own recipe app, learning all about the simplicity of SwiftUI along the way. We'll also learn about existing UI frameworks and how we can integrate those directly into our project with ease.

Once our iOS app is up and running, we'll see how making the transition over to iPadOS and watchOS is made even easier.

With brand new features built directly into Xcode 11 and the power of the Swift 5.2 programming language - SwiftUI is the start of something very special.

Who this book is for

This book is aimed at anyone, from a beginner to the world of iOS development, to an experienced Swift developer looking to get their hands on SwiftUI for the first time.

If you've been developing for other platforms, be it mobile, web, or APIs, and want to get stuck into something new, then this book is a great place to start.

What this book covers

Chapter 1, *Getting Started with SwiftUI*, offers an introduction to the Swift programming language and the SwiftUI framework.

Chapter 2, *Understanding Declarative Syntax*, provides details on declarative syntax and how this works in SwiftUI.

Chapter 3, *Building Layout and Structure*, discusses the architecture and design patterns that can be used with SwiftUI.

Chapter 4, *Creating Your First Application*, gives you an introduction to Xcode and shows how to create your very first project.

Chapter 5, *Understanding Controls, Views, and Lists*, is where we start to build a recipe app, learning about the core components available to us in SwiftUI.

Chapter 6, *Working with Navigation in SwiftUI*, sees us adding navigation to our recipe app and moving from one view to another.

Chapter 7, *Creating a Form with States and Data Binding*, covers how to create an input form and teaches you how to use states and binding.

Chapter 8, *Networking and Linking to Your Existing App Logic*, discusses adding a network layer and calling our app to retrieve data from an external source.

Chapter 9, *Maps and Location Services*, sees us working with MapKit and Location Services in SwiftUI.

Chapter 10, *Updating for iPad with NavigationViewStyle*, covers updating our recipe app to support the iPad.

Chapter 11, *SwiftUI on watchOS*, shows how to add a watchOS companion app to our recipe app.

Chapter 12, *SwiftUI versus UIKit*, covers comparisons between common UIKit and SwiftUI controls.

Chapter 13, *Basic Animation in Views*, touches on the basic animations available to us in SwiftUI.

Chapter 14, *Animations in Transitions*, allows you to learn how transitions work in SwiftUI alongside animations.

Chapter 15, *Testing in SwiftUI*, covers how to do UI and unit testing in Swift UI and looks at some of the debugging features available in Xcode 11+.

To get the most out of this book

In order to follow and code along with this book, you will need to own an Apple Mac that is capable of running macOS Catalina or later.

All the sample code examples have been tested on macOS Catalina 10.15.1, running Xcode 11.3. An understanding of the Swift programming language would be advantageous but is not essential.

In order to get the latest version of macOS Catalina, or to see whether your hardware supports it, please visit `https://support.apple.com/en-us/HT210222`.

To obtain the latest version of Xcode, please visit the Mac App Store and search for `Xcode` or visit the store at `https://apps.apple.com/us/app/xcode/id497799835`.

If you are new to iOS and macOS development and want to learn more about the Swift programming language, either prior to or after reading this book, I highly recommend *Mastering Swift 5* from Packt.

Download the example code files

You can download the example code files for this book from your account at `www.packt.com`. If you purchased this book elsewhere, you can visit `www.packtpub.com/support` and register to have the files emailed directly to you.

You can download the code files by following these steps:

1. Log in or register at `www.packt.com`.
2. Select the **Support** tab.
3. Click on **Code Downloads**.
4. Enter the name of the book in the **Search** box and follow the onscreen instructions.

Once the file is downloaded, please make sure that you unzip or extract the folder using the latest version of:

- WinRAR/7-Zip for Windows
- Zipeg/iZip/UnRarX for Mac
- 7-Zip/PeaZip for Linux

The code bundle for the book is also hosted on GitHub at `https://github.com/PacktPublishing/Learn-SwiftUI`. In case there's an update to the code, it will be updated on the existing GitHub repository.

We also have other code bundles from our rich catalog of books and videos available at `https://github.com/PacktPublishing/`. Check them out!

Conventions used

There are a number of text conventions used throughout this book.

CodeInText: Indicates code words in text, database table names, folder names, filenames, file extensions, pathnames, dummy URLs, user input, and Twitter handles. Here is an example: "Let's start by creating an instance of TableView in an empty ViewController."

A block of code is set as follows:

```
func tableView(_ tableView: UITableView, numberOfRowsInSection section:
Int) -> Int
func tableView(_ tableView: UITableView, cellForRowAt indexPath: IndexPath)
-> UITableViewCell
```

When we wish to draw your attention to a particular part of a code block, the relevant lines or items are set in bold:

```
class ViewController: UIViewController {

    var tableView: UITableView!
    override func viewDidLoad() {

        tableView = UITableView(frame: view.frame)
        view.addSubview(tableView)
    }

}
```

Bold: Indicates a new term, an important word, or words that you see onscreen. For example, words in menus or dialog boxes appear in the text like this. Here is an example: "Select **SwiftUI View** from the **User Interface** options and then click **Next**."

 Warnings or important notes appear like this.

 Tips and tricks appear like this.

Get in touch

Feedback from our readers is always welcome.

General feedback: If you have questions about any aspect of this book, mention the book title in the subject of your message and email us at customercare@packtpub.com.

Errata: Although we have taken every care to ensure the accuracy of our content, mistakes do happen. If you have found a mistake in this book, we would be grateful if you would report this to us. Please visit www.packtpub.com/support/errata, selecting your book, clicking on the Errata Submission Form link, and entering the details.

Piracy: If you come across any illegal copies of our works in any form on the Internet, we would be grateful if you would provide us with the location address or website name. Please contact us at copyright@packt.com with a link to the material.

If you are interested in becoming an author: If there is a topic that you have expertise in and you are interested in either writing or contributing to a book, please visit authors.packtpub.com.

Reviews

Please leave a review. Once you have read and used this book, why not leave a review on the site that you purchased it from? Potential readers can then see and use your unbiased opinion to make purchase decisions, we at Packt can understand what you think about our products, and our authors can see your feedback on their book. Thank you!

For more information about Packt, please visit packt.com.

Getting Started with SwiftUI 1

Here, we'll begin our journey into learning SwiftUI by building our very own SwiftUI app. We'll start by learning the history of the Swift programming language, which will act as a good foundation for understanding the core concepts of Swift development. Together, we'll build an app with custom animations and everyday elements that work seamlessly for iOS, iPadOS, and watchOS. From this, we'll see the benefits of writing good, clean code—once—for multiple devices. Once we have our working app, we'll cover testing and debugging, and see how crafting our code in the right way from the start can make this much simpler to implement.

We'll get started with the history of Swift before getting hands-on into Xcode, where we'll learn just how simple, yet powerful, developing in SwiftUI really is. In this chapter, we'll get you primed and ready for your journey into SwiftUI by first of all introducing you to the Swift programming language, along with the existing UIKit framework. We'll then discuss what SwiftUI brings to the table, and how it sits not only within a new project but in your existing projects too.

The following topics will be covered in this chapter:

- Introducing Swift as a programming language
- Learning about existing UI frameworks
- Introducing SwiftUI
- When to use SwiftUI, and why

Technical requirements

No technical requirements are needed for this chapter. We'll simply be going through an overview of Swift and SwiftUI; however, feel free to grab a coffee if you like!

Introducing Swift as a programming language

Whether you're a seasoned Mac/iOS developer or brand new to the scene, one way or another you'll have heard of Swift. The Swift programming language was first announced by Apple at the **Apple Worldwide Developers Conference** (**WWDC**) in 2014 and was intended to bring to the table numerous features from a multitude of other programming languages. Although not labeled as a successor, some feel that Swift was brought in to replace Apple's currently used programming language, Objective-C.

 Apple had actually been developing Swift since 2010, a project originally started by Chris Lattner, who joined Apple in 2005 to work on the **Low-Level Virtual Machine** (**LLVM**) toolchain project.

Since its announcement in 2014, Swift has taken on many iterations, with the current release at the time of writing being version 5.1.

However, the first major milestone for Swift came just after the announcement of version 2 at WWDC 2015, when Apple announced that version 2.2 was being open-sourced in December of that year. This decision was met with great enthusiasm by the community, with the ability to build, modify, and contribute to the Swift programming language. This kick-started many projects, including server-side Swift.

 Open source software—Software that is created and distributed by developers under specific licenses, such as Apache 2.0 GNU **General Public License** (**GPL**) and **Massachusetts Institute of Technology** (**MIT**). The different flavors of licenses determine how developers can use and distribute the software.

As mentioned previously, Swift was created with the idea of taking the best bits of other programming languages and rolling them into one.

Swift is known for providing benefits, such as being a type-safe language and its functional programming properties. For current macOS/iOS developers, one of the benefits of Swift is its ability to bridge and be used in conjunction with Objective-C, the benefit being that both languages use the LLVM compiler. The following screenshot shows an example of the type interface in Swift. As you can see, from *line 4*, there is no declaration of the type `String`; it is simply inferred by the value given:

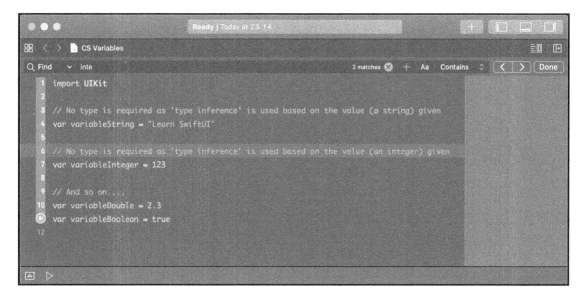

Another big win for Swift is that it allows developers to write *safe* code. If written correctly and by implementing the correct safeguards made available in Swift, a developer shouldn't have to worry about their application ever throwing errors. Safeguarding in Swift lets you validate against objects that could be *nil*, with a very simple and easy-to-read syntax, which can be seen in the following example:

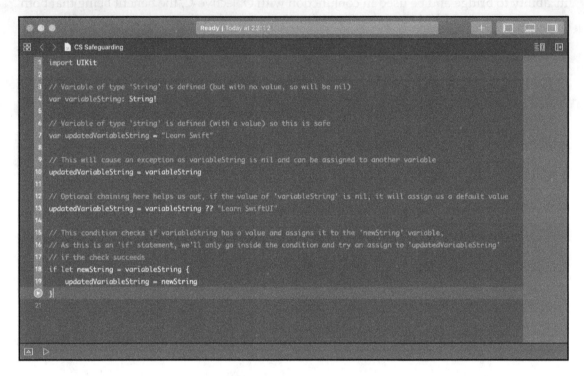

If you take a look at *line 18* in the preceding screenshot, you'll see that we check `variableString` to see if it's not *nil*—if so, then it's assigned to the `newString` constant and is now safely available for use within the `if` statement.

In this section, we learned about the history of the Swift programming language and some of its core features. Next, we'll learn about existing **user interface** (**UI**) frameworks made available to us in Swift.

Learning about existing UI frameworks

With all great programming languages come great frameworks—in particular, UI frameworks. In the case of Apple, UIKit has been the UI framework of choice since Objective-C, offering everything from labels, fonts, and buttons, to animation.

Written in Objective-C, UIKit has been the binding of the iPhone UI for all developers since the beginning. With a multitude of public APIs and documentation available to developers and solid support from the community, there has been little else to offer in terms of alternatives for Apple development.

Without UIKit, everyday interactions such as tap, pinch, and zoom gestures for drawing wouldn't be available. UIKit is even responsible for accessibility, which we'll touch on later on in this book.

The binding between UIKit and Swift can be performed in two ways: programmatically or through the Interface Builder.

Creating the UI programmatically

Creating the UI programmatically involves writing around five lines of code, such as in the following example:

```swift
import UIKit

class LearnSwiftUI: Any {

    @objc func onButtonTap() {
        // Do something cool!
    }

    func createButton() {
        let myFirstLabel = UIButton()
        myFirstLabel.frame = CGRect(x: 0, y: 0, width: 150, height: 75)
        myFirstLabel.backgroundColor = .blue
        myFirstLabel.titleLabel?.text = "Learn SwiftUI"
        myFirstLabel.target(forAction: #selector(LearnSwiftUI.onButtonTap), withSender: nil)
    }
}
```

As seen in the preceding screenshot, you first need to create an instance of the `UIButton`, set the frame (origin and size), set the background color, give the button's label some text, set a tap gesture (what happens when you tap the button), and then add the gesture to the button.

All this is done before we even place the button within our view hierarchy, not to mention writing the code to determine what happens when we tap the button.

All in all, quite a few lines of code—for something that could end up being a simple operation.

Creating a UI via Interface Builder

The second way is via Xcode's **Interface Builder**. Interface Builder is a built-in **graphical user interface** (**GUI**) that allows you to use either **XML Interface Builder** (**XIB**) files, **NeXTSTEP Interface Builder** (**NIB**) files, or Storyboards to design and create your layout with ease. With Interface Builder, you can simply drag and drop components such as Views (`UIView`), labels (`UILabel`), and Image Views (`UIImageView`) straight onto a canvas that can be wired straight into your code. The following is an example of how a button is created in Interface Builder and shows the code to handle the button's tap event:

Interface Builder was not always part of Xcode's **integrated development environment** (**IDE**). It was originally an independent application that ran in parallel with Xcode.

Although highly regarded by the Apple community, with the introduction of Swift UIKit slowly started to show its age. Swift's clean and compact syntax started to look bloated and untidy when asked to perform simple tasks, such as creating a frame for a button or performing an animation.

Many thought that this was simply how it was going to be from now on, with a focus on bringing UIKit to macOS deemed to be a greater necessity. But little did we know that Apple was about to change the way we build apps, for the foreseeable future.

In June 2019, at WWDC, Apple introduced us to SwiftUI.

Introducing SwiftUI

The Apple headline for WWDC 2019 was *We are going to blow your mind* and, indeed, they weren't wrong. As expected, many rumors floated around WWDC, with heavy conversations around Project Marzipan (which came to be announced as Catalyst), but no-one could have foreseen the announcement of a new UI framework—specifically, one built around Swift.

What is SwiftUI?

SwiftUI is a brand-new developer toolkit written in Swift for Swift. It presents a declarative syntax, allowing for more fluid and natural development along with more human-readable code.

It comes built into Xcode 11 and can be selected as an alternative to Storyboards when creating a new project. To include SwiftUI in your project, simply select this from the **User Interface** dropdown, as seen in the following screenshot:

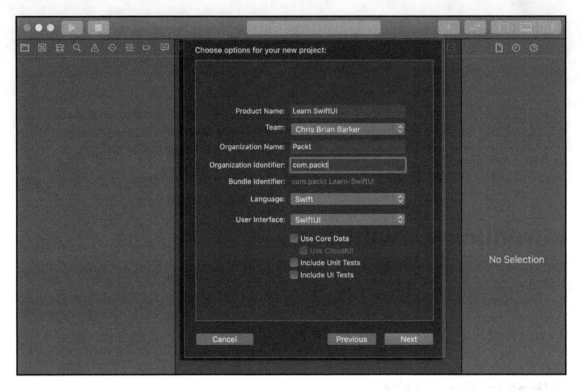

Compared to UIKit, SwiftUI allows you to move away from imperative programming (programmatically creating `UILabel` and `UIButton`, or dragging and dropping objects around Interface Builder) and gives you powerful interfaces that can be supported across iOS, iPadOS, macOS, watchOS, and even tvOS.

This approach to app development is a true cross-Apple platform and, along with the introduction of Catalyst, in just a few clicks your iPadOS app now becomes a true native macOS app—an option that simply wasn't available with UIKit.

Syntax in SwiftUI

SwiftUI makes full use of declarative syntax, which we'll go into further in much more detail in the next chapter, but the burning question on everyone's mind was *What's so special about declarative syntax?* Well, quite a lot, actually. Declarative syntax brings a whole new paradigm to writing and structuring UI-based code: no more dragging and dropping elements into NIBs and Storyboards, or complex constructors and properties to set, but more of an instruction (to the compiler)-based approach to generating and displaying UI elements.

First of all, forget about previous architecture patterns used in mobile apps (or any other object-oriented) development, such as **Model-View-Controller** (**MVC**), **Model-View-ViewModel** (**MVVM**), **Model-View-Presenter** (**MVP**), and so on. Delegate patterns commonly used in iOS/macOS development are no longer needed, as declarative syntax now makes use of States.

States and updating the UI

We'll touch on States in a later chapter but, as a general overview, if you assign `@State` to a property, SwiftUI will monitor this property and, if it is mutated or changed, will invalidate the current layout and reload.

Think of it in terms of a collection of data in a list. The data changes and the list is automatically updated and refreshed—no need to invoke a refresh call (or a `reloadData()`, as you might have previously seen in `CollectionViews` and `TableViews`).

Tools and features

Another powerful feature of SwiftUI is hot reloading—or the preview window, as it's called in Xcode. This allows you to make changes to your UI code in real time, without the need to build and rerun the app.

By creating a *Preview* struct inside your SwiftUI class, you can build and inject mock data, mock navigation, and images straight into your Xcode preview window. So, for example, a SwiftUI project might have a list that is dynamically populated by external data. This would allow you to inject dummy data into the preview window without running your app and calling an API.

Building for multiple devices

Whether you're building for iOS, macOS, iPadOS, tvOS, or watchOS, SwiftUI has you covered. All the features of SwiftUI can be built once and can support multiple devices, thus eliminating the need to write code multiple times.

In this book, we'll start by building an iOS app, which can be easily turned into an iPadOS app, followed by a watchOS app.

With UIKit, we had many options to build a cross-device UI right within Interface Builder, but this could often lead to complicated AutoLayout constraints, traits, or even size classes (which no-one ever really understood...).

 SwiftUI's standard library is written in Swift. However, its core foundation is actually written in C++ .

Next, we'll talk about the circumstances in which we may want to use or benefit from SwiftUI.

When to use SwiftUI, and why

When it comes to using SwiftUI, first off, you need to start by thinking of what type of app you're building. If you're looking to build the next shoot-em-up multiplayer game, then I'm afraid SwiftUI is not for you. However, anything else—from a banking app to a catalog app—can benefit immediately from Swift UI.

The afore mentioned declarative syntax allows for States to be used in order to allow effective but— more importantly—efficient reloads of data. For those familiar with UIKit's UICollectionViews or UITableViews, you'll know that writing logic to reload the whole table in order to change just one tiny value can be both tiresome and tedious.

Designers taking their first step into development will certainly benefit from SwiftUI, with top graphical design packages already rumored to be incorporating plugins that will allow SwiftUI syntax to be exported directly from the drawing board.

The term full-stack is often used (and overused) in the development industry, particularly with web developers. A frontend web developer would generally look after the design elements and visual construction of a site, such as HTML, **Cascading Style Sheets** (**CSS**), and presentation logic, with backend web developers concentrating more on core application logic, networking, and data layers.

This type of separation is not commonly seen in mobile app development, even though developers may follow the same, or similar, architecture patterns. Could SwiftUI be the first step toward acknowledging, and even achieving, full stack mobile app development?

As we'll find out in the next chapter, SwiftUI is perfect for beginners, either young or old. Interface and application logic can be written and designed in such a way it simply rolls off your tongue as you type, almost like painting by numbers.... but for developers.

Summary

In this chapter, we learned the history of Swift as a programming language, and how its first big milestone kick-started a now-thriving community. We then covered how UIKit was used alongside Swift to design and develop iOS apps and touched on its aging and complex syntax. The introduction of SwifUI came as a perfect companion to Swift, opening up avenues not just for seasoned developers but also for designers and people just starting their journey into the world of Apple app development.

Next, we are going to delve more deeply into the declarative syntax and talk about the benefits of this particular programming paradigm.

Questions

1. Which paradigms do SwiftUI & UIKit follow?
2. What was Swift's first big change?
3. What is open source software?
4. For which platforms can SwiftUI be developed?
5. Which UI GUI tools were used before SwiftUI?

Further reading

- **SwiftUI:** https://developer.apple.com/xcode/swiftui
- **WWDC:** https://developer.apple.com/wwdc19/
- **Declarative Programming:** https://en.wikipedia.org/wiki/Declarative_programming
- **Open Source Software:** https://en.wikipedia.org/wiki/Open-source_software

2
Understanding Declarative Syntax

In this chapter, you'll learn about the core fundamentals of the declarative syntax. You'll be able to identify and understand the theory behind it and the part it plays in SwiftUI development. We'll look specifically at how the syntax is written and how easily it can be intercepted and edited in a live debugging environment, all within Xcode. We'll finish off by going deeper into the structure of the syntax and understand how it all binds together. By the end of this chapter, you'll be able to fully understand what advantages are on offer, along with how to comfortably write a basic UI using declarative syntax.

Without declarative syntax, there would be no SwiftUI, or it would simply be another UIKit forcing users to learn a new framework with the same base language. Due to this, it is important to learn the fundamentals of the syntax as this will help you not only understand the core principles of SwiftUI but how to successfully utilize and build on the foundation that has been laid.

Learning SwiftUI without understanding its declarative syntax would be like trying to drive without really knowing what a car is and, although this does sound like a lot to learn before you've even written your first line of code, with this knowledge at hand, you'll be able to jump right into coding the syntax without any worries.

The following topics will be covered in this chapter:

- What is declarative syntax?
- Visualizing declarative syntax
- Nesting and decoration
- Imperative syntax

Technical requirements

For this chapter, you'll need to download Xcode version 11.3 or above from the Apple Mac App Store. You'll also need to be running the latest version of macOS (Catalina or above). Simply follow these steps:

1. Search for Xcode in the App Store and select and download the latest version.
2. Launch Xcode and follow any additional installation instructions that your system may prompt you for.
3. Once Xcode has been fully launched, you're ready to go!

What is declarative syntax?

In this section, you'll learn what declarative syntax is and what immediate benefit it offers for writing clean code. You'll also learn about its counterpart *imperative* syntax in order to gain understanding from both paradigms.

The declarative syntax is a programming paradigm that allows you to write code in a more formal and procedural way. In essence, the declarative syntax is a way of describing the code you want to write, without having to worry about how it's going to be implemented.

The following is an example of declarative syntax if it was said in spoken language:

> *"I would like a cup of tea, please"*

This is more of a statement than written logic as we are asking for something rather than being concerned about how we are going to get it.

Let's take our first look at SwitUI syntax. Here, we have created a Text Label with the value "Learn SwiftUI" and guess what... that's all we need to do:

```
Text("Learn SwiftUI")
```

As you may recall from Chapter 1, *Getting Started with SwiftUI*, and how we created Objects such as an instance of a UIButton or a UILabel, the example involves a lot less code; we don't need to jump through hoops to tell SwiftUI what we want to create – we simply ask for it.

Many languages already make use of declarative programming. A more commonly known language is the SQL syntax that's used in database queries and stored procedures.

The following is an example of a SQL stored procedure:

```
CREATE PROCEDURE SelectAllCustomers
AS
SELECT * FROM Customers
GO;
```

As you look at each line, you will see it's more of a statement than actual logic: you ask to `CREATE PROCEDURE`, without having to worry about how the creation is done, you `SELECT * FROM Customers`, without the need to get the Customer list, and even know how `SELECT` is performed for setup.

Now that we have a good idea of the concept behind declarative syntax and how it works as part of the programming paradigm, let's take a look at how we might use this in the real world by getting out project up and running in Xcode and seeing it for ourselves.

Visualizing declarative syntax

As we mentioned in the previous chapter, declarative syntax is used by many languages. A relatively recent framework, Google's Flutter, took on the declarative syntax approach and the wider developer community was immediately hooked. With this, it was only a matter of time before other frameworks started to follow.

 At the time of writing this book, Google has just announced Jetpack Compose for Android, which itself adopts the same approach to UI development.

Now, let's take our first steps into programming with SwiftUI. We'll start by getting to grips with Xcode, learn the basics of how to create a new project, and start to write our very first SwiftUI code!

Getting started with SwiftUI in Xcode

Let's start by opening Xcode and taking a look at how to set up our first SwiftUI project:

1. Start by opening Xcode.
2. Select **Create a new Xcode project.**
3. Select **Single View App.**
4. Finally, select **Next.**

Fill in the details as per the following screenshot while paying careful attention to the **User Interface**. SwiftUI should be selected for this:

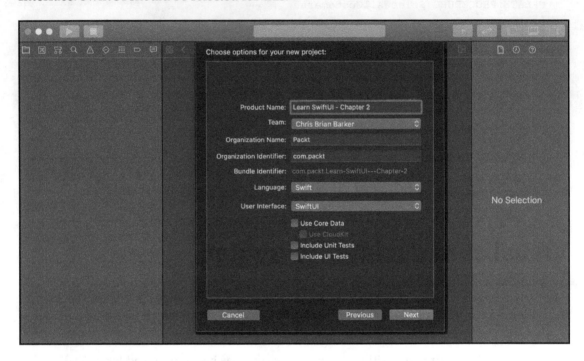

Also, note that **Team** will be different – if you've not set up Xcode before, you'll need select **Xcode** | **Preferences** | **Account** from the toolbar and add your Apple developer ID. If you don't have an Apple developer ID, you can register for one here: `https://developer.apple.com/`.

There are multiple types of Apple Developer account options, but, for the purpose of this book, you won't need a paid membership, although, if you would like to run your app on a physical device at some point, you will need either a standard Developer membership or an Enterprise membership. For more information on Apple Developer memberships, please go to the following link: `https://developer.apple.com/support/compare-memberships/`.

Now that we are all set up with our project, we can write out the first piece of SwiftUI and start to truly understand the declarative syntax. Next, we'll fire up Xcode for the first time and start building our very first application.

Making a "Hello World" app

Learning a new programming language always starts with "Hello World", no matter how experienced a developer you are (and I won't have anyone tell me any different).

SwiftUI is no different. By default, it will give you some very basic boilerplate code to get you started. If you followed the preceding sections correctly, you'll be presented with the following:

```
struct ContentView: View {
    var body: some View {
        Text("Hello World")
    }
}
```

This is your first look at SwiftUI's declarative syntax – looks great, doesn't it? Well, actually, it doesn't look like a lot, but when we break it down, you'll see how powerful it is and how much is actually being done.

Let's start by taking a look at the first couple of lines:

```
struct ContentView: View {
    var body: some View { }
}
```

What does this mean? Well, this is your main Content View for the *Single View App* you're about to create. In terms of UIKit, this is your main `UIView`, which may sit inside your existing `UIViewController` or simply be a view on its own. Everything that is going to be displayed on your screen will be returned in this one single view. We can, however, have multiple views being returned inside the body of `ContentView`, which leads us on to the next part – a `TextView`:

```
struct ContentView: View {
    var body: some View {
        TextView("Hello World")
    }
}
```

As you can see. there is a `TextView` inside our body that accepts a constructor of the `String` type. What we've done here is create a label with the text of `"Hello World"` and added it to our app, all with one line of code!

Notice how I said we were returning a `TextView` and I mentioned that we can return multiple views within our `ContentView` body, yet we appear to be missing the `return` keyword in front of our `TextView`. This is because SwiftUI (along with Swift 5.2) can now make use of implicit returns from single-expression functions.

 For more details on implicit returns from single-expression functions, take a look at the following read me from the open source Swift repository: `https://github.com/apple/swift-evolution/blob/master/proposals/0255-omit-return.md`.

Now that we've learned how to successfully return a single *View*, we can move on to returning more than one View. The next section is important as every element on a page in SwiftUI is of the View type and you will almost never return just a single View for your app.

Returning multiple views

Even with implicit returns, we can add multiple views to our body without the need for the *return* keyboard. First, let's try adding another TextView and see what happens:

```
struct ContentView: View {
    var body: some View {
        Text("Hello World")
        Text("Learn SwiftUI")
    }
}
```

Looking at the preceding example and trying to add another `TextView` underneath the existing one looks the right thing to do, but, unfortunately, if you duplicate the `TextView` in the current body, you'll be immediately presented with the following error:

```
Function declares an opaque return type, but has no return statements in
its body from which to infer an underlying type
```

Basically, this means that *body* is expecting a single return type of View, but we are passing back two Views (and it's not sure which one to use).

We solve this by first asking the question of how we want to display the text. If the desired effect is a list, then we simply make the following change:

```
struct ContentView: View {
    var body: some View {
        List {
            Text("Hello World")
            Text("Learn SwiftUI")
        }
    }
}
```

By wrapping our multiple Text views inside a List view, our body is again only being presented with one single view to which it can successfully compile based on its implicit return.

In this section, we've learned how to return multiple views that will form the foundations for many iOS and macOS applications. Next, we'll take a look at some more examples of other views we can create in SwiftUI, along with how to best handle nesting.

Nesting and decoration

Just from the examples in the previous section, you've seen the immediate benefit of not only SwiftUI but how it uses the declarative syntax to create Views and add them to your application.

In this section, we are going to dive a little deeper down the rabbit hole and look at how declarative syntax makes use of modifiers to decorate our Views and how to best handle adding multiple Views inside each other without getting into too much trouble.

Modifiers

Modifiers in SwiftUI are a simple yet effective way of rendering custom interactions and decoration. Let's take our previous example, add some basic modifiers, and see what we get:

```
struct ContentView: View {
    var body: some View {
        List {
            Text("Learn SwiftUI")
```

```
            .bold()
        }
    }
}
```

As you can see, we've added the `.bold()` modifier to our Text label, which does exactly what it says on the tin – it's made our text bold. It doesn't just stop there, though: as expected, you can add multiple modifiers to a View by simply chaining them together. Update your boilerplate code with the following to see the effect this has:

```
struct ContentView: View {
    var body: some View {
        List {
            Text("Hello World")
                .bold()
                .foregroundColor(.blue)
                .blur(radius: 1, opaque: false)
        }
    }
}
```

As you can see, we've added two additional modifiers, `foregroundColor` and `blur`. These built-in modifiers work as effectively as you would expect – take a look at the changes yourself by using the new Automatic preview pane in Xcode 11 that was built especially for SwiftUI.

On the right-hand side of your screen, you should see a canvas of the iOS simulator. If you can't and your changes are not automatically updating, you may need to press **Resume** on the top right:

```
       Learn SwiftUI  >   Learn SwiftUI  >   ContentView.swift  >  No Selection
 5  //  Created by Chris Barker on 25/10/2019.          Automatic preview updating paused  ⓘ   Resume
 6  //  Copyright © 2019 Packt. All rights reserved.
 7  //
 8
 9  import SwiftUI
10
11  struct ContentView: View {
12      var body: some View {
13          Text("Hello World")
14              .bold()
15              .foregroundColor(.blue)
16              .blur(radius: 1, opaque: false)
17      }
18  }
19
20  struct ContentView_Previews: PreviewProvider {
21      static var previews: some View {
22          ContentView()
23      }
24  }
25
```

Now, you should see the Automatic preview canvas with your text label decorated with the modifiers you've just added. In this instance, the text will be blue and bold, the label will have a blur around the text with a radius of 1, and it will not be opaque:

As we build our full SwiftUI app in the upcoming chapters, we'll cover many more modifiers and even how to create custom modifiers.

But first, let's dig a little deeper into the structure of declarative syntax and look at how nesting syntax is written and why it's important.

Nesting syntax

In this section, we'll cover nesting views within our main body view and learn when they are used. Believe it or not, we touched on nesting in the previous section. Remember when we added a List wrapper around our multiple Text boxes? That was nesting.

Let's have a look at some more examples of nesting in SwiftUI. First, we'll start off with our code from the previous section, which incorporated a List:

```
struct ContentView: View {
    var body: some View {
        List {
            Text("Hello World")
                .bold()
                .foregroundColor(.blue)
                .blur(radius: 1, opaque: false)
        }
    }
}
```

Next, we're going to add a Navigation view to our app since we want this to control the whole content of our app. To achieve this, we simply wrap NavigationView { } around the existing logic sat within our body:

```
struct ContentView: View {
    var body: some View {
        NavigationView {
            List {
                Text("Hello World")
                    .bold()
                    .foregroundColor(.blue)
                    .blur(radius: 1, opaque: false)
            }
        }
    }
}
```

As you can see, our new NavigatonView sits just inside of the body but wraps around our existing content (List and its Children).

And with that, we've successfully added a Navigation View to our app by nesting the existing content within a `NavigationView {}`.

Next, we'll take a look at grouping multiple Views together in SwiftUI.

Grouping

Grouping is a way of visually managing views within your code base. This can be performed very easily in SwiftUI by simply wrapping `Group {}` around your content within a `List` view, for example.

Try by adding the following to the code in the previous section and view the results in the Automatic preview window:

 I've removed the modifiers for this example as we'll be adding many more Text views shortly.

```
struct ContentView: View {
    var body: some View {
        NavigationView {
            List {
                Group{
                    Text("Hello World")
                }
            }
        }
    }
}
```

Let your Automatic preview windows update and take a look. What can you see? That's right – not much. Groups won't actually affect the way your UI is displayed as these containers are just a way for you (the developer) to order and add some structure, and allow you to visualize your syntax a little easier.

 As well as syntax aesthetics, you'll need to use Groups when returning 10 or more Views in one go as SwiftUI's `ViewBuilder` won't allow it.

In this section, we covered SwiftUI's syntax in a little more detail and started to understand the way it uses declarative syntax to structure code.

Imperative syntax

Imperative syntax is the more common form of programming that's used as it's much more functional and requires the programmer to write code that will tell the compiler how we are going to achieve the goal, rather than ask politely. The following is an example of imperative syntax:

> *"I would like some boiled water, a teabag, milk, and sugar. Allow the tea to brew for n minutes then add n teaspoons of sugar and n amount of milk...... oh and remove the teabag."*

Even with the preceding example, we could dig even deeper and say "*I need some water, then boil the water*" or "*type or brand of sugar*".

Let's take a look at the following Swift code. This is a typical class you may see when writing a standard Swift app. Take a closer look at the `makeBrew()` function and how each step is coded so that the compiler knows exactly what to do. This approach is imperative programming:

```swift
func makeBrew() {
    let brew = MakeBrew()

    brew.addTeabag(type: .earlGrey)
    brew.boil()
    brew.pourWater()

    DispatchQueue.main.asyncAfter(deadline: .now() + 120) {
        brew.addMilk(ammount: 11.0)
        brew.addSugar(ammount: 2)
        brew.stir()
    }
}
```

This is an effective class nonetheless, but there will potentially be a lot of code. This is not exactly UI logic, but this hopefully gives you a better idea about the structure of imperative syntax, especially when you compare it to SwiftUI's declarative syntax.

Summary

In this chapter, we learned how declarative syntax allows the developer to write syntax in a way that describes the actions and functions required and how its counterpart, imperative programming, is more logic-based.

We learned about the structure of declarative syntax and how understanding the view hierarchy is important to us, especially as every component on the screen is of the View type.

We also got to use SwiftUI for the first time in Xcode and took our first glance at the structure and arrangement that the declarative syntax has to offer, including nesting Views, and the importance of Group containers to arrange our subviews.

In the next chapter, we'll move onto the layout of SwiftUI and understand the structure of not just our code, but the architecture of our code base.

Questions

1. Describe declarative syntax.
2. What other syntax paradigms can we use?
3. What do modifiers do?
4. What visual effects do Groups have on our UI?
5. When are we forced to use Groups in SwiftUI?

Further reading

- **Declarative Programming**: https://en.wikipedia.org/wiki/Declarative_programming
- **SwiftUI View Modifier**: https://developer.apple.com/documentation/swiftui/viewmodifier
- **SwiftUI Groups**: https://developer.apple.com/documentation/swiftui/group

Building Layout and Structure

3

Now that we know a little bit about SwiftUI's syntax, let's look at how best to structure not only our code but also our project. In this chapter, you'll learn the importance of app architecture; we'll cover two of the most commonly used ones, **Model-View-View-Model** (**MVVM**) and **Model-View-Controller** (**MVC**), to see not only what they do, but also how we can adopt them in SwiftUI.

Learning about the importance of app architecture will allow us to not only understand but also visualize the separation of UI and application logic. More importantly, we'll learn how this separation will allow us to look closely at how SwiftUI works seamlessly with the new Combine framework in order to achieve a powerful yet efficient pattern.

The following topics will be covered in this chapter:

- UI logic – the MVVM architecture
- Design patterns in SwiftUI

Technical requirements

For this chapter, you'll need to download Xcode version 11.3 or above from Apple's App Store. You'll also need to be running the latest version of macOS (Catalina or above).

Simply search for `Xcode` in the App Store and select and download the latest version.

Launch Xcode and follow any additional installation instructions that your system may prompt you with. Once Xcode has fully launched, you're ready to go.

Download the sample code from the following GitHub link:

`https://github.com/PacktPublishing/Learn-SwiftUI`

Details will be given later on in this chapter about how to create your own Xcode project, should you wish to code along rather than reference the sample project.

Understanding UI logic – the MVVM architecture

In this section, you'll learn about how UI logic is separated from core application logic by taking your first look at the MVVM architecture pattern. MVVM is a widely used design pattern that allows us to separate core application logic from UI logic.

We'll go into the MVVM pattern in detail, which in turn will allow you to identify where SwiftUI should sit within a project.

MVVM overview

Let's start by looking at what MVVM actually has to offer. MVVM is a very popular and widely used architecture in the development industry alongside many others, including **Model-View-Presenter (MVP)** and **Model-View-Controller (MVC)**.

Although SwiftUI doesn't necessarily encourage a specific pattern, it doesn't mean you can't follow one yourself; MVVM particularly lends itself to SwiftUI.

Take a look at the following diagram. This is a standard MVVM pattern for a generic application:

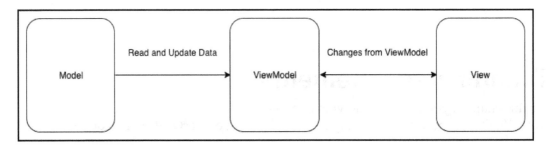

As you can see, there are three main components here. Let's take a look at each of them, going from left to right:

- **Model**: This is your core model, which will contain all data that you may have consumed from a database or via an external API.
- **ViewModel**: A stripped-down or UI-tailored representation of your Model that contains only the information required for your View.
- **View**: The interface/UI that will be presented to the user and will harness the data from your `ViewModel`.

The beauty of this is that it allows separation of responsibility between code and logic. The logic that determines how the View is rendered sits in once place and is not tightly coupled to anything else other than its own concerns. The core application logic, which can include algorithms and network requests, can sit away from this and work independently.

There are so many more benefits from this that are beyond the scope of this book but we'll cover testing in later chapters, where we'll see the advantages of this pattern again.

Now that we understand the basics of the MVVM architectural pattern and have covered some of its benefits, let's compare SwiftUI's architecture with that of the MVVM pattern.

MVVM in SwiftUI

Although SwiftUI is provisionally a UI framework, apps being built in SwiftUI will mostly be written in SwiftUI's syntax, so architecture patterns are just as important.

Looking back at the MVVM diagram in the previous section, how does a SwiftUI project sit within this pattern and do we need to make any changes to the way we work?

The answer is: NO, not really. SwiftUI conforms nicely to this pattern, which you can see in the following diagram:

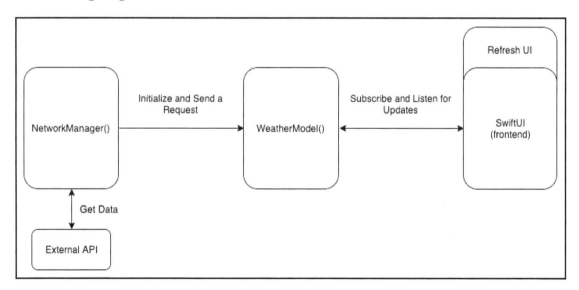

As you can see from the diagram, the pattern is almost identical to the diagram for the MVVM pattern we saw earlier. From right to left, we have our SwiftUI frontend, which is bound via a subscription (we'll cover that in later chapters) to our `WeatherModel()`, and then we finally have our `NetworkManager()`, which is responsible for our external API call.

In the next section, we'll take a look at a sample SwiftUI project that conforms nicely to the MVVM pattern, but first let's look at another popular architecture pattern and see how this compares to SwiftUI and MVVM.

Other architecture patterns

MVVM is a great way to get started with SwiftUI, but there are many other patterns, and you might not always have the luxury of starting a project from scratch. So, let's take a look at another very common pattern, MVC, which doesn't necessarily fit into SwiftUI's design patterns. Comparing MVC to SwiftUI will allow us to identify SwiftUI's place in a project:

- **Model**: Responsible for housing your user data
- **View**: The UI presentation, displaying data bound from the Model
- **Controller**: Your application logic, the link between the View and the Model

So, why doesn't this work for SwiftUI? Well, there are two reasons, really:

- In `Chapter 2`, *Understanding Declarative Syntax*, we saw how SwiftUI uses the declarative and not imperative syntax and how unnecessary application logic is no longer needed: by simply *asking* what we want. This logic, would have made up a good portion of Controllers (or helpers or manager classes that were called from our Controller).
- SwiftUI uses states and object binding, so there is no longer a need to have logic in Controllers that controls and updates our UI; SwiftUI handles all of this for us.

 We mentioned states and bindings in `Chapter 1`, *Getting Started with SwiftUI* and touched on them in the preceding SwiftUI MVVM diagram. We'll go over how the pattern fits into the application architecture later in this chapter, before fully implementing it in our first app later on in the book.

As we just learned, MVC is a very simple yet powerful design pattern and is still used by many to this day, but by comparing it to SwiftUI we can now start to get a better understanding of where SwiftUI sits in a day-to-day application.

In the next section, we'll learn how the MVVM pattern applies to SwiftUI.

Design patterns in SwiftUI

Now that we've compared two of the most common design patterns and we can see where SwiftUI fits within them, we'll take a deeper look at how we can actually write SwiftUI to conform to one of these patterns. In this section, we'll cover what a binding is and how this helps us adhere to the MVVM pattern. We'll also cover states, which show why Controller logic in MVC has no place in SwiftUI.

Observable objects

Next, we are going to look at observable objects, and by observable we mean models that can change state or be updated due to an external API call. For example, a model that houses weather information from a weather API might get updated periodically. We would want our UI (or SwiftUI, in our case) to monitor this model for any changes and implement updates accordingly.

To dig a little deeper into how MVVM works with SwiftUI, let's write a small application that takes some data from an external API, parses the data, and then displays the data within our app.

`ObservableObject` is a protocol that is part of the new Combine framework, which was announced alongside SwiftUI at WWDC 19. Combine is Swift's own version of Reactive Streams, and it enables objects to be monitored (observed) and data to be passed through streams from core application logic back up to the UI layer. For example, a network request that could take *n* amount of time to retrieve data can be observed and, when ready, pushed back asynchronously to the UI layer, which will be updated accordingly. Before Combine, RxSwift was a very popular open source framework used for Reactive Streams.

You'll find a link to a full working sample project for you to use as a reference at the beginning of this chapter. The project is called `MVVM - Chapter 3`. Simply download or clone the GitHub link and double-click the file called `Chapter 3 MVVM.xcodeproj`. This will launch Xcode.

Create a new project by clicking **File** | **New** | **Project**, select **Single View App**, and click **Next**. Choose a product name (anything you like). Making sure **SwiftUI** is selected for **User Interface**, click **Next** and then **Create**.

See the following screenshot for a look at the options you'll be presented with during this process:

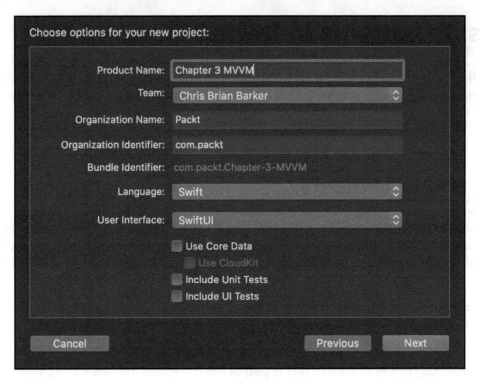

Great! We're off, and you can now follow along using the following snippets and the files from the sample project. Let's start by having a look at the sample project you just downloaded. Open the folder and double-click on `Chapter 3 Architecture.xcodeproj`. This should load the project in another Xcode window.

You'll notice the file tree on the left-hand side containing all our Swift files for the project. Notice how there are three group folders under `Chapter 3 Architecture`:

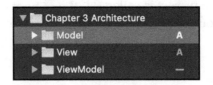

I've separated out the relevant files into groups corresponding to their place in the MVVM architecture. Let's start by taking a quick look at each one and we'll pinpoint certain parts of code that are important:

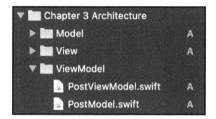

This is one of our ViewModels (the VM in MVVM), responsible for holding the data that we'll show in our View (our main UI). You'll notice that one of the first functions written is actually an initializer:

```
init() {
    getPosts()
}
```

This means that whenever the `PostViewModel` class is initialized, the `getPosts()` private function is called. Let's take a look at `getPosts()` and see what it does:

```
private func getPosts() {
        guard let url = URL(string:
        "https://jsonplaceholder.typicode.com/posts")
        else {
                return
            }
        NetworkManager.loadData(url: url) { articles in
            if let articles = articles {
                self.articles = articles.map(PostModel.init)
            }
        }
    }
```

Basically, this logic makes a call to `NetworkManager` (also included in our project tree, as `NetworkManager.swift`) with a URL and returns some dummy JSON data.

Once the data is returned, it's bound using Swift's Codable protocol to a global variable in our class called `articles`. The `articles` variable is a list (an array) of `PostModel`, which we'll look at next and will be the source of data for our View.

Codable is a way to bind JSON data (or dictionaries) to models/classes/objects in Swift. First made available in Swift 4, Codable takes away the labor of manually binding and safeguarding a JSON response. For more information and to learn about Codeable in Swift, see the following documentation at Apple's developer portal: `https://developer.apple.com/documentation/swift/codable`.

Codable is another `ViewModel`, which is responsible for holding all the data for our required View. The data comes from the response, where we decide what to populate our view with.

Let's take a closer look. Click on the `PostModel.swift` file:

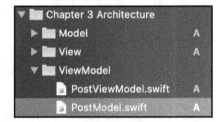

Take a look at the contents; there are a couple of things to pay attention to:

```
init(article: PostResponse) {
    self.post = article
}
```

The initializer shown in the preceding snippet accepts a type of `PostResponse`. This a **Model** (the M in MVVM) and is the decoded JSON response that comes back from the call our `NetworkManager` made. Don't worry too much about how all that works right now. The `PostResponse` value passed in is assigned to a local variable called `post`.

Next, you'll see a list of computed properties:

```
var title: String {
    return post.title ?? ""
}

var description: String {
    return post.body ?? ""
}
```

These computed properties allow us to assign values from our `post` variable and manipulate them should we wish to (although all we do here is some basic inline safeguarding).

Now we know how all those pieces fit together, let's take a look at one more very important thing; we'll head back over to our `PostViewModel` class. Following is the `articles` public variable we mentioned before. You'll notice something different about it from a standard variable:

```
@Published var articles = [PostModel]()
```

That's right: the `@Published` attribute—but hold that thought and we'll see how this all links up and why it's important in the next section.

To recap, we've so far learned how Models and ViewModels sit within a SwiftUI project and, more importantly, how and why they work together.

Publishing objects

This is where things start to get exciting...

Let's start by taking a look at our SwiftUI View; you'll find this under the `View` group in the file tree:

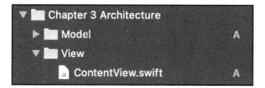

First of all, let's take a look at the code in the body and go through exactly what's going on here:

```
var body: some View {
    List(model.articles) { article in
        VStack(alignment: .leading) {
            Text(article.title)
            Text(article.description)
                .foregroundColor(.secondary)
        }
    }
}
```

Just after the `body` variable is declared, we see the `List` property being used, which requires a list (an array) of objects that we can iterate through. In this instance, we pass it a copy of our `PostModelView` (which has been declared as the `model` variable in this class). As we saw earlier, this has a property called `articles`, which is an array of `PostModel`.

The SwiftUI list will iterate around the `model.articles` array and in turn assign a variable called `article` to each iteration. Each `article` variable can then be used to populate each section of our list view.

As you can see from the preceding snippet, we also add a `VStack` instance inside our list. `VStack` allows us to create the direction of the content we are going to display. V is for *vertical*; if we wanted to go horizontally, we would use `HStack`.

Now we know how our data is displayed, and previously we looked at how we get and parse data. Now let's work out how we link the two together. Still inside the `ContentView.swift` file, let's take a look at the previously mentioned `model` variable:

```
@ObservedObject var model = PostViewModel()
```

Again, do you notice anything different from your standard variable declaration? That's right! The `@ObservedObject` attribute: this means the variable will listen to changes from within the `PostViewMode` class, changes that are published from within.

Jump back to `PostViewModel.swift` and let's quickly remind ourselves of the `@Published` attribute we saw on the `articles` property.

So, when our API returns a value and assigns it to `articles`, this will tell the `PostViewModel` class that something has changed and anything listening for this change (in our case, `@ObservedObject` in `ContentView.swift`) will update accordingly. We'll also need to make sure that our `PostViewModel` conforms to `ObjectObservable` too, thus allowing it to become a class that can be observed:

```
class PostViewModel: ObservableObject {
```

Now that might seem all well and good, but just because our `model` property has been updated with a new value, how does the SwiftUI know to reload the list? After all, the data could take 5 seconds to get from the external API and at this point, the main `ContentView` will have already loaded.

This is where SwiftUI's states come into play. With `ObservableObject`, any changes to the property will force SwiftUI to reload the body, thereby eliminating any need to programmatically worry about reloading data. This is just another fine example of declarative programming.

Summary

We've learned a lot in this chapter. First, we looked at the importance of app architecture and the separation of UI logic and application logic. This was a fundamental building block in our understanding of how SwiftUI's framework sits within an app architecture. Next, we covered MVVM and MVC and compared them to see how SwiftUI fits (and doesn't fit) into these structures. We learned that MVC has no place in SwiftUI due to its use of controller logic, which is not really needed in SwiftUI.

Then, we looked at a sample project that made good use of the MVVM architecture. By looking at the code and how the responsibilities of each class were laid out, we were able to easily see the role of SwiftUI with the app. Also, this pattern allowed us to explore and understand object binding, which is part of the Combine framework released alongside SwiftUI.

In the next chapter, we'll start to take everything we've learned from the first three chapters and begin to build our very own recipe app – all in SwiftUI.

Questions

1. Name two common architecture patterns.
2. What architecture pattern doesn't fit the SwiftUI way of working?
3. What is the ViewModel responsible for?
4. What does our ViewModel need to conform to in order to become observable?
5. Which framework do Publish and Observable belong to?

Further reading

- **Combine Framework:** https://developer.apple.com/documentation/combine
- **MVVM Architecture**: https://en.wikipedia.org/wiki/Model%E2%80%93view%E2%80%93viewmodel
- **RxSwift:** https://github.com/ReactiveX/RxSwift

Summary

Questions

Creating Your First Application

4

In this chapter, we'll begin to code our very first app in SwiftUI – exciting, I know, but before we learn to run, we need to walk a little further first. The Xcode IDE will play a fundamental role in our journey, so we'll cover the basics and core components in a little more detail. We'll look at how Xcode allows us to write our SwiftUI code and give us almost immediate feedback. We'll also touch on how and, more importantly, why we may need to use the iOS simulator to run our app in certain scenarios.

The following topics will be covered in this chapter:

- Xcode, as an IDE
- Core components of Xcode
- Mock data in Automatic Preview

Technical requirements

For this chapter, you'll need to download Xcode version 11.0 or above from the Apple Mac App Store. You'll also need to be running the latest version of macOS (Catalina or above).

Simply search `Xcode` in the App Store and select and download the latest version. Launch Xcode and follow any additional installation instructions that your system may prompt you for. Once Xcode has been fully launched, you'll be ready to go.

Xcode, as an IDE

In the previous chapters, we covered some of the fundamental basics elements of Swift, SwiftUI, and the application architecture. In those chapters, we touched on Xcode, Apple's **integrated development environment** (**IDE**) for creating iOS, iPadOS, watchOS, and macOS applications. Many different frameworks and programming languages use various IDEs – Android developers may use the Android Studio IDE, Java developers will most commonly use Eclipse, and .NET Microsoft developers will use Visual Studio.

As you can probably tell by Xcode's latest version (11), it's been around for a while and is exclusive to macOS. While you can use other programming languages such as C and C++, Xcode is predominantly used for core Apple development.

In this chapter, we'll have a closer look at Xcode and get to know the IDE a little better. We'll cover various menu options, shortcuts, and debugging tools, all in preparation for the next chapter, where we'll start writing our very first iOS app in SwiftUI.

Creating our first project

It's time to create our very first project! We touched on this back in Chapter 3, *Building Layout and Structure,* but let's take a closer look at some of the options we're presented with when creating a project and why they are important.

Let's get started by performing the following steps:

1. Launch Xcode.
2. Go to **File** | **New** | **Project**.
3. Select **Single View App** and click **Next**.
4. For **Product Name**, type My Favourite Recipes.
5. Make sure **SwiftUI** is selected for the **User Interface**.

Now, before we go any further, let's go through these options and find out what each one means:

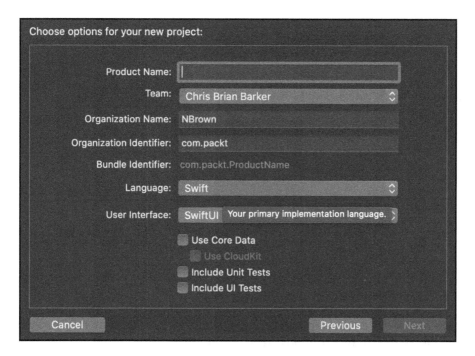

- **Product Name**: This is the name of your project (not to be confused with the name of your app).
- **Team**: As per `Chapter 1`, *Getting Started with SwiftUI*, you'll need to register for an Apple developer account. You can be registered for more than one account and have these linked in Xcode. There is a little more to all of this, but this is out of the scope of this book.
- **Organization Name:** The name of your company, the company you are writing your app for, or simply just your name.
- **Organization Identifier**: This is an identifier that will be used to generate the Bundle ID of the app. Once published, an app's Bundle ID cannot be changed, nor can it be used by anyone else – so choose wisely. The standard practice for choosing a Bundle Identifier is using a reverse domain name service notation such as `com.packt.learn-swift-ui`.

- **Bundle Identifier**: This will be automatically generated from the **Product Name** and the **Organization Identifier.**
- **Language**: You have the option of Swift or Objective-C (we'll need Swift for SwiftUI).
- **User Interface**: Options for SwiftUI or Storyboards (UI Kit approach). We'll be choosing SwiftUI.

You'll see the following additional options:

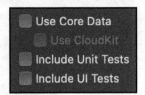

We don't need to worry about these just yet, so just leave them unticked, but rest reassured we'll touch on these in a later Chapter 15, *Testing in SwiftUI*.

Click **Next**; you'll be now asked to select a location to save your project; this can be anywhere you like. Once selected click **Create**

Now that we've got our project up and running, you'll be presented with a template, similar to what we saw in the previous chapters. Now, let's take a look around and see what Xcode has to offer.

Core components of Xcode

Much like many other IDEs, Xcode has a plethora of options and tools to choose from. In this section, we'll cover some of the basics and firm favorites that may seem familiar with other IDEs and have been there from the start, as well as some that are specific to SwiftUI. Unlike many other IDEs, Xcode doesn't rely on (or allow even) third-party extensions or plugins, thus making all its features not only safe but reliable.

Navigator

The Navigator (or the file tree, in some cases) is a common component in many IDEs and Xcode is no different. The Navigator can be found on the left-hand side of the interface and offers options such as filtering, search and replace, errors and warnings, debugging options, and many more:

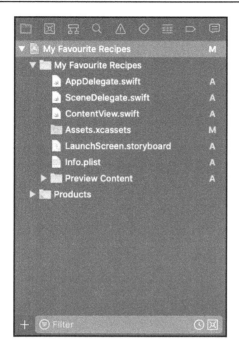

As you can see, there are multiple tab options within the Navigator. We'll cover these as/when we need to during the course of this book, but it's good to know they are there.

Scheme and device list

Next, let's take a look at the scheme and device list, which can be found at the top of Xcode. In a nutshell, the scheme (on the left-hand side of the picture) is your app. At this stage, that's all you really need to know.

The following is what you should see for your scheme and device list in Xcode:

Devices, when clicked, will give you a list of available iOS simulators that you can use to run your app. Also, if connected, your iPhone or iPad will show up in this list too, allowing you to debug and run your application directly on a physical device. For the majority of this book, we'll be running all our applications on a simulator or more excitingly, we'll be using the brand new **Automatic Preview** option that was introduced with Xcode 11 and macOS Catalina.

Automatic Preview

Xcode 11 brought us a lot of new features, but one of the most exciting ones was that of the Automatic Previewer, which is built directly into the Xcode 11 IDE.

Automatic Previewer sits to the right of the Xcode IDE and allows us to preview the changes we are making in SwiftUI without the need to run the simulator, as shown here:

As shown in the preceding screenshot, this is the Automatic Preview window in its initial state; nothing has been run yet. Let's look at what happens when we press **Resume**:

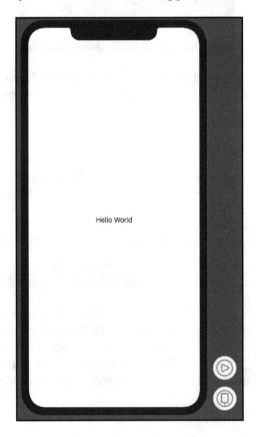

Within a few seconds, a simulator is loaded into the canvas and our template `"Hello World"` application is loaded. Now for the exciting stuff: let's make a change to the SwiftUI code and see what happens.

In the file tree, single click on the `ContentView.swift` file and make the following change in our SwiftUI's **Body** property:

```
var body: some View {
    List {
        Text("Hello World")
        Text("Learn SwiftUI")
    }
}
```

Did you notice something strange? If you copy and pasted the preceding code, you should have instantly seen the Automatic Previewer update to show a **List** view and the new line.

If you typed out the code, you will have seen this update in real-time as you were typing – awesome!

Xcode Simulator

The Automatic Previewer is a fantastic new addition to Xcode 11 and is specifically for building interfaces with SwiftUI, but, when the time comes to test your application with core logic such as networking or switching between screens, you'll need to call on the power of the Code Simulator.

Going back to the device list next to the scheme bar we saw earlier, select a simulator you would like to test against and then press the play button to the left of it.

After an initial cold boot, your selected simulator will load and your application will launch automatically:

By default, Xcode will give you a list of available simulators current to the SDK you're building against, but additional simulators can be downloaded for testing on legacy devices, such as iPhone 6S, iPhone SE, and so on, all with earlier versions of iOS installed on them.

In this section, we covered some of the core components that Xcode 11 has to offer that we'll be using throughout this book, including the Automatic Previewer. Next, we'll go a little deeper into the workings of the Automatic Previewer and how we can programmatically mock data to produce a dynamic preview of the view we are building.

Mock data in Automatic Preview

As we mentioned in the previous section, the Automatic Preview window is a brand new feature for Xcode 11 and macOS Catalina. It allows you to view your UI changes without the need to launch the simulator and reload the application. In this section, we'll take a look at how we can mock data that we will inject into our View in order to preview our UI changes with simulated content, but, more importantly, we'll cover why this is important.

Understanding Automatic Preview

Automatic Preview will no doubt play a big role as you venture into the world of SwiftUI as you'll be able to create your content with the ease and beauty of SwiftUI's declarative syntax and the ability to see your changes hot-reload instantly in front of you. But the ability to inject mock data at the same time will not only save you time but let you effectively make structural designs with ease.

Let's start by taking a look at what we mean by this. In your new project, update your `body` with the following code:

```
var body: some View {
    Group {
        VStack {
            List(recipeNames, id: \.self) { name in
                Text("\(name)")
            }
            List(recipeModel.recipes, id: \.self) { name in
                Text("\(name)")
            }
        }
    }
}
```

Here, we have a Group since we are going to return two **Lists** nested inside a **Vertical-Stack** (**VStack**). The first List is going to iterate around a global array called `recipeNames` within our struct, while the second will iterate around a List that is coming from an external source via a model called `recipeModel` (which we'll simulate for the purpose of this example).

So, we'll start by creating our two data sources. Add the following code just above the body declaration:

```
let recipeNames = ["Italian Pizza Chicken",
                   "Greek Pasta Bake",
                   "Hearty Parsnip Soup"]
@ObservedObject var recipeModel = RecipeModel()
```

As we mentioned previously, the first is a simple array of recipes – it's local to the **struct** we are working in. The second is obtained from a model that will get the data from an external source.

Let's take a quick look at `RecipeModel()`, just for reference:

```
class RecipeModel: Identifiable, ObservableObject {
    @Published var recipes = [String]()
    var id = UUID()
    init() {
        DispatchQueue.main.asyncAfter(deadline: .now() + 3.0) {
            self.recipes.append(contentsOf: ["Pork & Potato Hotpot",
                                             "Thai Green Curry",
                                             "Italian Sausage & Beans"])
        }
    }
}
```

Here, we have a nice simple model following the Observable pattern that we covered in the previous chapter.

Note that in `init()`, we are not actually making an external API call. This is because, for the purpose of this example, we are going to simulate it by simply creating another hardcoded array (with different values), but with a delay around it, thus simulating a callback from a server. There are other ways to simulate API calls; for example, we could also stub out a closure, but this is effective enough for now.

Let's get back to our `ContentView.swift` file. Let's click **Resume** on the Automatic Previewer. What do we see?

That's right – only our top values are shown. This is because Automatic Preview will only render the data it has available at the time of rendering the **View**; that is, when the View is initially rendered, the data from our `RecipeModel()` is not ready. We can test this theory by hitting play in the top left of Xcode and running our code in the simulator, as follows:

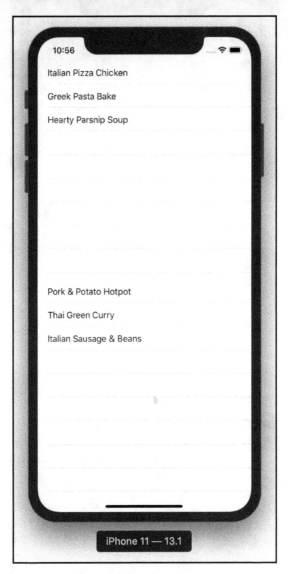

And there we go – both our lists are showing as expected, but what do we do if all our data is coming from an external source? We don't really want to hardcode values within our struct just for testing. This is where `PreviewProvider` comes in.

Understanding the Preview Provider

`PreviewProvider` is brand new to Xcode 11 and specifically new to SwiftUI. By creating a struct that conforms to the `PreviewProvider` protocol (which sits within your SwiftUI class; for example, `ContentView.swift`), along with a couple of lines of code, Xcode will automatically generate a preview of your SwiftUI View.

As we've seen so far, using the Automatic Preview window is a real treat, but there are a couple of scenarios that we need to be aware of.

So, let's start by stripping back our project a little. While removing the hardcoded values, make the following changes to the struct:

```
struct ContentView: View {
    var recipeNames = [String]()
    var body: some View {
        VStack {
            List(recipeNames, id: \.self) { name in
                Text("\(name)")
            }
        }
    }
}
```

Here, we're simply amending the app to iterate around a list of `String()` since there is no data. We can't see what or how the View is going to be displayed. This is where `PreviewProvider` comes in. Take a moment to familiarize yourself with the following code:

```
struct ContentView_Previews: PreviewProvider {
    static var previews: some View {
        ContentView()
    }
}
```

The preceding struct is responsible for generating the preview we can see in the Automatic Preview window. By creating a struct that conforms to the `PreviewProvider` protocol, we can simply create a static variable that returns our `ContentView()` struct.

With the preceding changes, click **Resume** in the Automatic Preview window. As expected, you'll see that nothing is displayed on the screen other than an empty list. Now, let's add some mock (or test) data via `PreviewProvider`.

Update your code to the following:

```
struct ContentView_Previews: PreviewProvider {
    static var previews: some View {
        ContentView(recipeNames: ["Italian Pizza Chicken",
                                  "Greek Pasta Bake",
                                  "Hearty Parsnip Soup"])
    }
}
```

As with all structs, you can instantiate an object by supplying a value to the properties that sit within them (in this case, the `recipeNames` variable). Here, we constructed our variable and passed in our mock data. Our Automatic Preview window should update automatically. If it doesn't, press **Resume** and you'll see our mock data appear.

Summary

In this chapter, we started our very first application and took a deeper look around Xcode as an IDE, along with the fundamental changes that were made specifically for SwiftUI. We touched on schemes and device lists, but most importantly, the Automatic Preview window.

We also learned how SwiftUI uses the Automatic Preview window and covered scenarios when it doesn't, in which case we would have to revert back to the iOS simulator.

In the next chapter, we'll look at some of the commonly used UI controls (such as text and images) and how to apply them within our app.

Questions

1. What does IDE stand for?
2. Why would the Automatic Preview window not display our data?
3. How do we inject mock data to display content in the Automatic Preview window?

Further reading

- **Xcode**: https://en.wikipedia.org/wiki/Xcode
- **Reverse Domain Name Notation:** https://en.wikipedia.org/wiki/Reverse_
  domain_name_notation
- **Swift Documentation – Classes and Structures**: https://docs.swift.org/
  swift-book/LanguageGuide/ClassesAndStructures.html

Understanding Controls, Views, and Lists

5

User interaction plays a big part in all apps; from pressing buttons to gestures, images to switches, Apple takes care of it. While creating interactions programmatically has always been an available option, taking advantage of out-of-the-box system controls has never been easier. Along with the help of Apple's Human Interface Guidelines, SwiftUI makes this even easier.

In this chapter, we'll learn how to add buttons, images, and segmented pickers to our app—we'll see how easy it is to decorate our controls with the simple use of modifiers. We'll also look at creating custom views that allow us to reuse a specific View in multiple areas of our app, without the need for code duplication. We'll go deeper into the automatic previewer and see how we can reuse mock data that has been previously created to work on our specific custom View.

By the end of this chapter, you'll have a much clearer understanding of how controls work within SwiftUI, and specifically, how they fit into the everyday life of an iOS app and how to continue to adhere to Apple's Human Interface Guidelines.

The following topics will be covered in this chapter:

- Exploring and understanding `Text` and decoration
- Custom Views in Lists
- Adding more controls

Technical requirements

For this chapter, you'll need to download Xcode version 11.3 or above from the Apple Mac App Store. You'll also need to be running the latest version of macOS (Catalina or above).

Simply search for Xcode in the App Store, and then select and download the latest version.

Launch Xcode, and then follow any additional installation instructions that your system may prompt you for. Once Xcode has fully launched, you're ready to go.

Exploring and understanding Text and decoration

In the last chapter, we started to build the skeleton of our very first SwiftUI app, and in this section we are going to take this a little further and continue to build upon the app. We'll take our basic List and then expand on the various Text options that are available to us in SwiftUI, along with how we can add images to our List that are not only stored locally, but also dynamically from an external source.

Finally, we'll dig a little deeper into modifiers in order to help decorate our app. By adding those little bells and whistles, we'll start to see how the little things that we do make our app feel more intuitive.

Text options

We've covered the Text() object in a couple of chapters now, but there is so much more to show, so let's head straight back to the code that we left in Chapter 4, *Creating Your First Application*:

```
var body: some View {
    VStack {
        List(recipeNames, id: \.self) { name in
            Text("\(name)")
        }
    }
}
```

As we can see, the `Text` View is just a basic control (along with a string being interpolated). Let's start by making some small amendments; then we can see what options are available to us. For the next code snippet, we'll just focus on the `Text` object for now:

```
Text("\(name)")
    .font(.headline)
```

Directly after the `Text` object, press *Enter* and then type `.font(.headline)`. Here, we are adding a font modifier to our object and passing in a pre-defined `.heading` font style. If your Automatic Preview window has not already updated, press **Resume**. Notice anything new? That's right, your font has now changed to bold, as shown in the following screenshot:

As previously shown, the font modifier accepts a parameter type of `Font()`; here, we could simply pass in a font that we've created programmatically (such as a custom font that we've acquired externally), but a neat little addition to SwiftUI allows us to choose from multiple pre-defined fonts, just like `.heading`, which we used previously.

If you hover over the `.heading` property in the previous code and press **command**, single-click, and then select **Jump to Definition**, you'll be presented with the definition file that has been taken from the public header, which exposes all of the APIs that are available for developers to use.

Some of the current pre-defined font types that SwiftUI offers are shown here:

```
/// Create a font with the large title text style.
public static let largeTitle: Font

/// Create a font with the title text style.
public static let title: Font

/// Create a font with the headline text style.
public static var headline: Font

/// Create a font with the subheadline text style.
public static var subheadline: Font

/// Create a font with the body text style.
```

```
public static var body: Font

/// Create a font with the callout text style.
public static var callout: Font

/// Create a font with the footnote text style.
public static var footnote: Font

/// Create a font with the caption text style.
public static var caption: Font
```

Have a play around with the various options and see how they look in the Automatic Preview window.

Next, let's style up our List a little. Underneath the current `Text` object, let's add another and style this accordingly. In the following example, we've added a couple of basic `font` modifiers to our `Text` Views:

```
Text("\(name)")
        .font(.headline)
Text("\(name)")
        .font(.subheadline)
```

So, as you'll see from the Preview window, we've duplicated the `Text` View, but our second view now has a slightly different style. Let's improve the layout a little by wrapping the two views inside a VStack, as shown here:

```
VStack {
  Text("\(name)")
  .font(.headline)
  Text("\(name)")
  .font(.subheadline)
}
```

There we go, our `Text` Views are nicely wrapped inside our VStack.

Code indentation works great in Xcode when going from one line to another, however, if you ever get yourself into a mess, simply highlight the selected area that you need to adjust, and press *Ctrl + I*, which will format your code accordingly.

Next, we'll update `PreviewProvider` to reflect the changes that we've made.

Updating PreviewProvider

Your Automatic Preview will now show a nice stacked cell with both a headline-styled font and a sub-headline-styled font. But our app isn't going to show duplicate recipe names as we've created so far, so we'll now adjust the model that we created in Chapter 4, *Creating Your First Application*, in order to accept a sub-heading.

Make the following change to RecipeModel.swift:

```
struct RecipeModel: Identifiable, Hashable {
    var id = UUID()
    var name = ""
    var origin = ""
}
```

We've really stripped this down so that it is a basic model passing in just a unique ID and name and origin properties. Next, we'll update ContentView.swift to reflect this change, as shown here:

```
var recipes = [RecipeModel]()
var body: some View {
    VStack(alignment: .leading) {
        List(recipes, id: \.id) { recipe in
            VStack {
                Text("\(recipe.name)")
                    .font(.headline)
                Text("\(recipe.origin)")
                    .font(.subheadline)
            }
        }
    }
}
```

Noticeable changes have been highlighted in the preceding code, but these are mainly just changes to the model name and to the properties that we'll access while we iterate around a recipe in our array of RecipeModel().

Next, we'll need to update our PreviewProvider struct. As you'll probably already have seen, nothing is showing up, so we'll need to make a couple of changes. Make the following amendment to your code and then let's go through it:

```
struct ContentView_Previews: PreviewProvider {
    static var previews: some View {
        ContentView(recipes: ContentPreviewHelper.mockRecipes())
    }
}
```

So, the noticeable changes that we have made here are the parameter name that `ContentView` accepts, and we've also added a call to a function that will create our mock data (which, in turn, returns an array of `RecipeModel()`). Let's now go ahead and add that helper function:

```
struct ContentPreviewHelper {
    static func mockRecipes() -> [RecipeModel] {
        var recipes = [RecipeModel]()
        recipes.append(RecipeModel(id: UUID(), name: "Italian Pizza
                                   Chicken", origin: "Italian"))
        recipes.append(RecipeModel(id: UUID(), name: "Greek Pasta Bake",
                                   origin: "Greek"))
        recipes.append(RecipeModel(id: UUID(), name: "Hearty Parsnip Soup",
                                   origin: "British"))
        recipes.append(RecipeModel(id: UUID(), name: "Honey & Soy Salmon",
                                   origin: "Chinese"))
        return recipes
    }
}
```

Taking a look at the preceding code, we simply create an empty array of recipes and then, line by line, we add the mock data that we want to display in our Automatic Preview window.

Go ahead now, and click **Resume** in the Automatic Preview window, and you should see our mock data being displayed just as we expected.

Next, try and run the app on our simulator. What do we get? That's right, there's no data shown; that's because our app, as it is stands, is not actually being passed any data—we're just using `PreviewProvider` to simply mock the data in Xcode.

A little more Text decoration

Now that we've got some more structure to our app, we can go back and add a little more decoration. Start by adding the highlighted modifiers to our `Text` Views and see what happens, as shown here:

```
Text("\(recipe.name)")
    .font(.headline)
    .foregroundColor(Color.blue)
Text("\(recipe.origin)")
    .font(.subheadline)
    .foregroundColor(Color.purple)
```

You should now see the following change in your Automatic Preview canvas:

Again, as you can see, a simple addition to each `Text` View makes such a difference– don't forget to use our previously mentioned **Tip** to see all of the options that are available to us in SwiftUI.

`.forgroundColor` accepts a `Color` type, which is new to SwiftUI (previously, this would have been `UIColor()` in `UIKit()`); you can pass in custom colors by creating an extension.

Let's try another one. Make the following highlighted amendments to your `Text` Views, and see what changes are made:

```
Text("\(recipe.name)")
    .font(.headline)
    .foregroundColor(Color.blue)
    .bold()
Text("\(recipe.origin)")
    .font(.subheadline)
    .foregroundColor(Color.purple)
    .italic()
```

Again, by adding two very simple one-line modifiers, SwiftUI allows us to make very quick changes that immediately have a big impact on our app.

In this section, we have covered the use of `Text` Views within our SwiftUI application, and how to add simple modifiers to decorate our app. Next, we'll go a step further and look at creating custom cells within our List views, which gives us more control over the content that we have created, and will aid us un the reusability of our code.

Creating custom Views in Lists

In this section, we'll take a look at how we can create custom and re-usable views to use in our List View. It's important that we understand the value of doing this early on, as it reduces the need for code duplication; while SwiftUI's declarative syntax is visually appealing, too much code in your struct can be daunting and very unnecessary.

Creating a custom view

First, let's start by creating another custom view, which, in turn, will house our layout and logic for each row. At the bottom of the `ContentView.swift` file, create the following struct in the format that would create a View struct for SwiftUI:

```
struct RecipeView: View {
    var body: some View {

    }
}
```

We've called this struct `RecipeView`, and as per its name, it will contain all the UI logic that is needed in order to display the recipe information that is required for our List View.

Next, let's populate this with the code that we previously created in the *Exploring and understanding Text and decoration* section. Let's start by highlighting the area in the following code that we are going to extract, and learn a little about which bits we need to leave in, and why:

```
var body: some View {
    VStack(alignment: .leading) {
        List(Recipes, id: \.id) { Recipe in
            VStack {
                Text("\(recipe.name)")
                    .font(.headline)
                    .foregroundColor(Color.blue)
                    .bold()
                Text("\(recipe.origin)")
                    .font(.subheadline)
                    .foregroundColor(Color.purple)
                    .italic()
            }
        }
    }
}
```

As you can see from the preceding code, we've highlighted everything inside, including the VStack. This is because this logic sits within the List iteration and it is generated for each row that is created. This is the logic that we could potentially want to reuse at a later stage, but more importantly, the separation will allow us to work on the row independently away from our core View's logic.

Let's now take the preceding logic and add this to our new struct. This can be seen in the following code:

```
struct RecipeView: View {
    var recipe: RecipeModel
    var body: some View {
        VStack(alignment: .leading) {
            Text("\(recipe.name)")
                .font(.headline)
                .foregroundColor(Color.blue)
                .bold()
            Text("\(recipe.origin)")
                .font(.subheadline)
                .foregroundColor(Color.purple)
                .italic()
        }
    }
}
```

Once again, we've highlighted the changes that have been made, and as you can see, we've simply lifted the VStack and its contents and added it to our View's body. Notice the addition of the `recipe` variable above the body declaration. This is required as our new View isn't aware of our recipe model from previous Views; it's completely agnostic to anything we've worked with before, therefore, **RecipeView** will need to accept this parameter in order to display the values.

Now that `RecipeView` has been created, let's hook this up back in our main View, and watch the magic unfold:

```
var body: some View {
    VStack(alignment: .leading) {
        List(Recipes, id: \.id) { recipe in
            RecipeView(recipe: recipe)
        }
    }
}
```

And it's a simple as that; by replacing our VStack and its contents with the initialization of our View (along with passing the iteration of our `recipe` model across), we've created a reusable view. If the Automatic Preview window has now already updated, press resume, and you'll see our test data be injected and the rows will appear as expected.

Working independently with our new custom view

Now that we've successfully created our own custom view, let's take this a step further and extract this into its own file, so that we can work on this independently should we ever need to. To do that, follow these steps:

1. Create a new file in our Xcode project called `RecipeView`, by highlighting the group name in the file tree, then right-click and select **New File**:

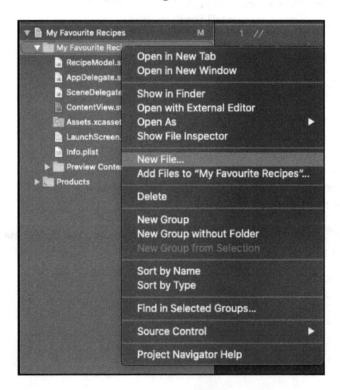

2. Select **SwiftUI View** from the **User Interface** options and click **Next**. Call your new file `RecipeView.swift` and click **Create**.

   Once you've done that, you should see some boilerplate code again, however, you'll be presented with the following compiler error: `Invalid redeclaration of 'RecipeView'`. This is simply because we've already created a View called `RecipeView` in our `ContentView.swift` file.

3. Head back over there, and take a copy of the contents of the `RecipeView` struct, and then delete the entire struct as we'll no longer be needing it.

   Now, go back into `RecipeView.swift`, and pass over the boilerplate code that has been generated; your struct should now show something like the following code:

```
struct RecipeView: View {
    var recipe: RecipeModel
    var body: some View {
        VStack(alignment: .leading) {
            Text("\(recipe.name)")
                .font(.headline)
                .foregroundColor(Color.blue)
                .bold()
            Text("\(recipe.origin)")
                .font(.subheadline)
                .foregroundColor(Color.purple)
                .italic()
        }
    }
}

struct RecipeView_Previews: PreviewProvider {
    static var previews: some View {
        RecipeView()
    }
}
```

Once you've done that, our refactoring is almost done and ready to go. However, there is a slight difference; highlighted in the preceding code is the `RecipeView` initializer in our newly generated `PreviewProvider`. In turn, this should be throwing the following compiler error: **Missing argument for parameter 'recipe' in call**. This is because our boilerplate generated a preview in order to initialize `RecipeView` without any arguments, and as `var Recipe: RecipeModel` isn't optional, we are forced to add a parameter.

4. Let's temporarily silence the error; to do so, we'll initialize the variable as shown here:

```
var recipe = RecipeModel()
```

The problem is gone; now move over to our automatic Preview window and press **Resume**.

5. If the Automatic Preview window is not present, click on the following icon, which can be found in the top-right corner of Xcode, and select **Canvas** from the List:

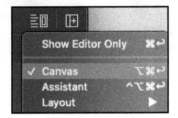

Once built, you should see the familiar sight of the simulator running inside of Xcode, but there is something missing... that's right, there's no data. The reason for this is because we've moved our new view away from `ContentView.swift`, which will initially execute the core layout of our app (in which we have already injected test data via its own `PreviewProvider`).

6. Now, we are simply just looking at a single line in our List, but that doesn't mean we can't add custom data into that, too. Make the following change to `PreviewProvider` in `RecipeView.swift`:

```
struct RecipeView_Previews: PreviewProvider {
    static var previews: some View {
        RecipeView(recipe: RecipeModel(id: UUID(), name: "Italian
                                  Pizza Chicken", origin: "Italian"))
    }
}
```

7. Click **Resume** in the preview window—our test data should be injected nicely and our view will be visible.

The first thing that you'll notice is that our view is being centered and not right-aligned as we would expect. This happened because our view is being tested in isolation from our other code. In other words, it doesn't know its intention is to be displayed as a row in a List. We can fix that easily by wrapping `RecipeView` inside a List view right within `PreviewProvider`, as shown here:

```
struct RecipeView_Previews: PreviewProvider {
    static var previews: some View {
        List {
            RecipeView(recipe: RecipeModel(id: UUID(), name:
                "Italian Pizza Chicken", origin: "Italian"))
        }
    }
}
```

Again, press **Resume** (if not already updated) and you'll see our single row displayed as it would be in our List view. We could go the extra mile with our preview and duplicate the code that was used to generate our List from `ContentView.swift` right within `RecipeView_Previews`. From this we can then call our `mockRecipes()` helper that we previously created, and pass the same data across (giving us more consistency with our test data throughout our app). Go on, have a go and see how you get on. (Refer to the sample code if you get stuck.)

In this section, we have covered how to refactor and reuse our code throughout our app, and the importance of this. We also touched on how we need to adjust our mock data in order to accompany creating a view independently from our main UI logic, and how, if it is done correctly, we can achieve a consistent structure throughout the app.

Adding more controls

Now that we have a solid foundation for getting our app off the ground, let's experiment with some more controls that are available for us to use in SwiftUI. We've already touched on some of the basic controls, such as Text and Button, but from a UI perspective. We can add some really valuable user interaction not only by adding controls into our app for the user, but by changing how controls easily and seamlessly interact with the way we handle data in our app.

Buttons

Let's start by adding a Button to our app that has an image. The reason that we want Buttons—rather than just an image—is that we want the user to be able to interact with this control, which not only performs an action, but can also change the state of our app.

Let's start by heading over to our `RecipeView.swift` file and we'll work from there. To start with, make the following highlighted changes to the code, and we'll go through them one by one:

```swift
var body: some View {
    Group {
        VStack(alignment: .leading) {
            Text("\(recipe.name)")
                .font(.headline)
                .foregroundColor(Color.blue)
                .bold()
            Text("\(recipe.origin)")
                .font(.subheadline)
                .foregroundColor(Color.purple)
                .italic()
        }
        VStack(alignment: .trailing, spacing: 10) {
            Button(action: {
                self.recipe.favourite.toggle()
            }) {
                Image(systemName: self.recipe.favourite ? "star.fill" : "star")
            }
        }
        .frame(minWidth: 0, maxWidth: .infinity, minHeight: 0, maxHeight: .infinity, alignment: .trailing)
    }
}
```

Let's go through the preceding code in more detail. First, notice that we've wrapped our existing `VStack` inside a `Group`; we covered this in `Chapter 2`, *Understanding Declarative Syntax*, in that a Group is required when a View is required when returning more than X amount of rows in a List. In this case, it is the same principle as when returning multiple Stacks (whether that is HStacks or VStacks).

Second, we've added the previously mentioned second VStack and created a Button inside it—let's take a closer look at how we created the Button.

As you can see from the previous example, the Button has an action closure; basically, this allows any code within this closure to be executed when the Button is pressed (more on the code inside the closure shortly). Next is the View (or Views) that we are going to display within the Button; in this case, we've added in an image.

We can set an image by simply passing in the name (as a string) of an image that we have inside the app's bundle or asset catalog, but as we've not yet added any images to our app, we're going to use a new feature called SF Symbols.

SF Symbols are system images that are available in iOS/macOS developments, which we can use anywhere inside our app. There is a wide variety of images available, including symbols in many different states (**off** and **on**, **empty** and **fill**, and so on). In this case, we are going to use star and star.fill.

Before we go any further, we need to make a quick change to RecipeModel; head over to RecipeModel.swift, and add in the following highlighted property:

```
struct RecipeModel: Identifiable {
    var id = UUID()
    var name = ""
    var origin = ""
    var favourite = false
}
```

We've now created a Boolean value for a property called favourite, and we've used type inference again to set the default value to false.

Go back to RecipeView.swift, and make the following highlighted the change to the RecipeModel variable:

```
@State var recipe = RecipeModel()
```

We've added the @State attribute to the variable, which, as we learned in a previous chapter, allows Swift UI to reload our app, based on the changes that are made to anything on that property.

Next, let's have a closer look at the code that is used to create our Button. As part of the action, you'll see us reference a .toggle() method on our newly created favorite property. Toggle is a Swift function that will switch our Boolean to its opposite value (based on its current value).

Next is the image view we've added in. Notice that we do more than just reference the SF Symbol image; we've used ternary logic to determine the current state of the `favorite` property—if the value is true, we show the `star.fill` image. If the value is false, we show the **star** image —nice and simple, but more importantly, clean and easy to understand.

As a result of the previously mentioned changes, we have created a Button that will toggle a property's value when it is pressed, as the property is part of `RecipeModel`, which we bound with the `@State` attribute. If a change is made, SwiftUI will invalidate the layout and re-draw—at this point our ternary logic will kick in and show us a different image based on the new value. Let's give it a go.

Now, for this we'll need the live simulator as we can't interact with objects in the previewer. Go ahead, and run the simulator on your desired device.

 Keyboard shortcuts are a quick and easy way to build or run apps within Xcode. *command + B* will build your app, *command + R* will run your app in the selected simulator.

What do you notice? That's right, nothing shows—that's because our app isn't passing any real-life data in. All we are seeing is the mock data that we use for the automatic previewer. For now, we'll put a quick workaround in—make the following change in `ContentView.swift` and rerun the app again, which will allow us to inject our mock data while the app is running via Xcode:

```
#if DEBUG
var recipes = ContentPreviewHelper.mockRecipes()
#else
var recipes = [RecipeModel]()
#endif
```

Basically, we've used a macro to check if our app is running in debug mode (when running via Xcode to the simulator, it will almost always be in debug mode).

If the app is indeed running in debug mode, we'll use our previously written helper to inject some mock data into our variable.

Run the app again, and you should now see some content. Go on, click on the stars, what do you notice? That's right, with the click of each star, we can now easily and efficiently toggle the state of them; and by efficiently, I mean compared to `TableView` or `CollectionView` in UIKit, where we would have to programmatically reload the view once we identified a change in behavior—nice!

Images

Adding images to use in an Xcode project has never been easier, whether that's downloading them remotely from an API or accessing them locally. In this part, we'll concentrate on adding images locally to the project, which can then be bundled as part of the binary. Follow the steps given here:

1. First, head over to the project that was created specifically for this chapter (you don't need to open Xcode, just access it via Finder on your Mac).
2. Inside the subfolders look for a file called `Assets.xcassets`.
3. Copy this file, and head over to your project (again via Finder), locate your `Assets.xcassets`, and paste (choosing to replace, when prompted).
4. Now, back in Xcode, locate `Assets.xcassets` in the file tree and highlight it.

   To the right of the file tree, you should see a List of images, specifically flags. These images are now bundled and ready to use in our app, so let's head over to `RecipeModel.swift`, and add the following property:

   ```
   var countryCode = ""
   ```

   We've added in `countryCode`, which we'll pass across in our `mockData()` function, and from this we'll match up the country code with the name of the images that we have just added in.

5. Now, go back over to our `RecipeView.swift` file and make the following highlighted amendment:

   ```
   VStack(alignment: .leading) {
       Text("\(recipe.name)")
           .font(.headline)
           .foregroundColor(Color.blue)
           .bold()
       Image(recipe.countryCode)
   }
   ```

   Notice how we've removed the second `Text` View and replaced this with an image view; nice and simple, we simply just reference the `Assets.xcassets` name of the image, and SwiftUI does the rest.

If you try and build now, you'll get a compiler error, any idea what this may be? That's right, we're missing the `countyCode` parameter from our test data; amend the constructor of each mock item to the following:

```
RecipeModel(name: "Italian Pizza Chicken", origin: "Italian", countryCode:
"IT")
RecipeModel(name: "Greek Pasta Bake", origin: "Greek", countryCode: "GR")
RecipeModel(name: "Hearty Parsnip Soup", origin: "British", countryCode:
"GB")
RecipeModel(name: "Honey & Soy Salmon", origin: "Chinese", countryCode:
"CN")
```

If not already updated, press the **Resume** Button on the automatic preview window.

And just like that, we've added in the corresponding country flag with just one line of code in `RecipeView`—so simple, yet very effective.

Segmented (picker) contols

Segmented controls (or a picker with the style of `SegmentedPickerStyle`, as they are called now) have been around for a long time in iOS development, often mistakenly referred to as tab selectors (or selectors). The aim of segmented controls is to allow us to shift from one view to another, all within a single screen. We'll create one in our application in order to allow us to switch between two Lists—one List with all our recipes and another for our favorites.

First, we need to create a `Helper` class along with a couple of functions that will allow us to achieve this. Don't be too concerned about the actual logic in this Helper, although we'll go over it at a higher level in order to understand what exactly is happening. Follow the steps given here:

1. Create a new file in our Xcode project called `RecipeView`—highlight the group name in the file tree, right-click, and select **New File**.

2. Select **Cocoa Touch Class** from the **Source** options and click **Next**. Call your new file `Helper.swift` and then click **Create**. Next, paste in the content from the same source file that was downloaded in the sample project—we'll go through each method one at a time to touch on what they do:

   - `addRemoveFavourite()`: Adds or removes favorites based on recipe name and whether they are already persisted (saved) or not.

- getFavourites(): Gets an array of RecipeModel that contains our favorite recipes.
- isFavourite(): Checks if a favorite or a specific recipe name already exists.
- mockRecipes(): Taken from our previously created function in ContentView.swift, the subsequent function can now be removed (remember to change the struct reference, though).

3. Now that we have set that up, let's look at making some changes to our app in order to support a segmented picker; head on over to ContentView.swift and make the following changes:

```
@State private var viewIndex = 0
var body: some View {
    VStack {
        Picker(selection: $viewIndex, label: Text("")) {
            Text("Recipes").tag(0)
            Text("Favourites").tag(1)
        }.pickerStyle(SegmentedPickerStyle())
        if viewIndex == 0 {
            List(recipes, id: \.id) { recipe in
                RecipeView(recipe: recipe)
            }
        } else if viewIndex == 1 {
            List(Helper.getFavourites(), id: \.id) { recipe in
                RecipeView(recipe: recipe)
            }
        }
    }
}
```

Let's go through the preceding code, starting with the viewIndex variable. We create this in order to observe and reference the current state of our picker as we move from one section to another. Because we added the @State attribute, any changes will result in SwiftUI reloading our View.

Next, we create the picker. Notice how we set $viewIndex as the selection (this will default to the 0 indexes, as per our default value that we set). Next, we set the labels that we require; for now, we are just going to use Text, so we add one for our current recipes and another for our favorites. Finally, we add a .pickerStyle modifier and set this to the SegmentedPickerStyle() type.

Once we've got our picker set up, we can now add conditional logic in order to determine which List with which data will be shown, based on the currently selected picker. With our previous code snippet, `viewIndex == 0`, we'll show our existing List. However, if `viewIndex == 1` then we'll show our List view, but instead of our mock data, we'll pass in a List of our persistent favorites.

Now, head back over to `RecipeView.swift`, and let's take a look at our existing `Button` logic. We'll need to make a few minor changes here in order to persist when a recipe is persisted or removed. Make the following highlighted changes to your `Button` view:

```
Button(action: {
    Helper.addRemoveFavourite(recipe: self.recipe)
    self.recipe.favourite.toggle()
}) {
    Image(systemName: Helper.isFavourite(name: recipe.name) ? "star.fill" :
"star")
}
```

Let's go through the changes in the preceding code. On the action of our Button we'll call our new `Helper` function, which will add or remove the recipe to our List of favorites.

Next, we'll use our new `isFavourite()` function to determine the logic for our ternary operator.

As you can see, we're still toggling `self.recipe.favourite` in order to update our state, which, in turn, will force SwiftUI to reload. This is not really necessary, as we don't reference `self.recipe.favourite` anymore, but we'll clean this up later on.

And that's all we need to do—run your application now in the iOS simulator and have a play; you should be able to star favorites and view these in a separate List. If you re-launch the app, you'll see that your favorites are still persisted and that the stars are already filled, where applicable.

Summary

In this chapter, we started by changing the style of our Text View by using pre-defined font styles that are available to us through SwiftUI. Using our fonts in this way allows us to easily keep a consistent look throughout the app, with very little effort. Next, we looked at how to add color and how to amend the weight of our Text with the use of modifiers. From this, we added another Text View and saw that by using a VStack, we could obtain our desired look.

In order to preview our data without the need to launch the app in the simulator, we updated `PreviewProvider` with mock data, thus allowing us to easily identify how our View would look and feel.

After we added text to each row in our List View, we extracted this in order to make it reusable throughout the app. This is an important subject in app development, as some Views can easily become either very complex or are required to be reused in other areas. By extracting the view, we eliminated the risk for code duplication, and also used the mock data that was created previously in order to style our View independently.

Finally, we delved into some other commonly used controls—we looked at Buttons and again, we saw the beauty of how SwiftUI uses states in order to accompany an action taken on a Button press. This was more apparent when we looked at segmented controls, and again, we hooked up a state variable that listened for interactions from within the control and adjusted our layout accordingly.

In the next chapter, we'll cover navigation, which plays a massive part in most iOS apps. It's something that is mostly taken for granted, as it easily appears to be the natural way of getting around an app.

Further reading

- **SF Symbols:** https://developer.apple.com/design/human-interface-guidelines/sf-symbols/overview/
- **Adding Images to Xcode** https://developer.apple.com/library/archive/documentation/Tools Languages/Conceptual/Xcode_Overview/AddingImages.html
- **Apple Human Interface Guidelines** https://developer.apple.com/design/human-interface-guidelines/

Working with Navigation in SwiftUI

6

In this chapter, we'll really start to bring our app to life by adding another View that will list our recipe in full, along with ingredients and instructions. From this, we'll learn the importance of navigation in our app, which, in turn, will allow us to tap into our existing recipe lists and populate and view our recipe in full.

This approach will require us to pass data from one View to another, which we'll cover when adding our Views to a navigation stack. From this, we'll introduce the use of `EnvironmentObjects`, which allow our Views to share objects globally, yet only requiring us to initialize and inject data once.

The following topics will be covered in this chapter:

- Creating additional Views
- App navigation
- Accessing with `@EnvironmentObject`

Technical requirements

For this chapter, you'll need to download Xcode version 11.3 or above from the Apple Mac App Store. You'll also need to be running the latest version of macOS (Catalina or above).

Simply search for `Xcode` in the App Store and select and download the latest version.

Launch Xcode and follow any additional installation instructions that your system may prompt you for. Once Xcode has fully launched, you're ready to go.

Creating additional Views

More often than not, apps have more than one page—in our previous chapter, we used a cool way of switching between our lists using a segmented style picker, but for pages that visually and logically look different, we require a completely different view.

In this section, we are going to create a dedicated page for our recipe. We'll use Image Views (for a picture of our recipe), Text Views for our recipe details, and we'll revisit `PickerView` and look at the alternative options that this affords us.

Creating the recipe details View

We'll start by creating a new SwiftUI View. We'll create a new file in our Xcode project called `RecipeDetailView` by highlighting the group name in the **File Tree**, right-clicking and selecting **New File**. Select **SwiftUI View** from the **User Interface** options and then click **Next**. Call your new file `RecipeDetailView.swift` and click **Create.**

Our details view will allow us to view the ingredients and recipe details of a selected dish. There will be a bit more code in here than our previous files, but don't worry; we'll go through the code one change at a time. First, let's start by adding the following two properties to our new struct:

```
@State var recipe: RecipeModel!
@State private var viewIndex = 0
```

The `RecipeModel` single model will contain the details of our recipe that we'll use to populate the data in our view. `viewIndex` will serve the same purpose as it did in the previous chapter as, again, we'll be using a segmented control in this view.

The following code snippets will be inside our `var body:` some View declaration. We'll go through these one at a time and they should be added to your project in this order:

```
VStack(alignment: .leading, spacing: 15) {
    // Image (currently using flag)
        Image(recipe.countryCode)
            .resizable()
            .aspectRatio(contentMode: .fit)
            .frame(maxWidth: .infinity, maxHeight: 200)

    // Remaining code will go here...
}
```

Start by adding a VStack (as per the comment, the remaining code will nest inside here too). Inside the VStack, we add an Image view. For now, we'll reference the flags we previously added to our project—if you recall, their names in our `Assets` folders matched the `countyCode` property in our `RecipeModel`, so we'll reference that from our previously declared variable.

Next, we'll add some modifiers to give us the behavior we require. Setting `resizeable()`, `.aspectRatio(contentMode: .fit)`, and `.frame(maxWidth: .infinity, maxHeight: 200)` will fill the image to the width of the screen, setting a predefined height along with a ratio that fits the screen (without cropping).

We'll now add two Text views in order to display our recipe name and its origin. Notice that the main difference here (other than the values we use) lies in the font modifier:

```
HStack {
    // Name of our recipe
    Text("\(recipe.name)")
        .font(.title)
        .padding(.leading, 10)
    // Favourites Button
    Button(action: {
        Helper.addRemoveFavourite(recipe: self.recipe)
            self.recipe.favourite.toggle()
            }) {
        Image(systemName: isFavourite ? "star.fill" : "star")
        }
    }
// Recipe origin
Text("Origin: \(recipe.origin)")
    .font(.subheadline)
    .padding(.leading, 10)
```

We are also going to pinch our Favourites Star button from `RecipeView.swift`. Now that we've seen how the logic works, we can move it into its new home in `RecipeDetailView` (and you can remove this from `RecipeView.swift` too).

If you take a closer look at the implementation of the star image, you'll notice that we have a property called `isFavorite`. Here, we've created a property called a 'computed property'—think of this as a shortcut to a small amount of logic that's not quite enough to be in its own function.

Add the following highlighted computed property alongside the existing store property:

```
private var isFavourite: Bool {
    return Helper.getFavourites().contains(where: {($0.name ==
recipe.name)})
}
```

This computed property gives us a much cleaner way of checking whether our current recipe is a favorite by rechecking our persisted helper data.

Next, we'll add another picker view with the style of a segmented control. So, just like we did in the previous chapter, we'll create a new Picker view—that references the previously created `viewIndex` state variable:

```
// Picker to choose between Ingredients & Recipe
Picker(selection: $viewIndex, label: Text("")) {
    Text("Ingredients").tag(0)
    Text("Recipe").tag(1)
}.pickerStyle(SegmentedPickerStyle())
```

Notice here again that we have two options for our picker, `"Ingredients"` and `"Recipe"`.

Now, let's add the logic based on what will appear when each segmented control is shown. I've highlighted here the main logic for each index:

```
// Logic to determine which Picker View to show.
if viewIndex == 0 {
    List(recipe.ingredients, id: \.self) { ingredient in
Image(systemName: "hand.point.right")
        Text(ingredient)
    }
    .listStyle(GroupedListStyle())
} else if viewIndex == 1 {
    Text(recipe.recipe)
        .padding(15)
        .multilineTextAlignment(.leading)
}
```

For the first index, we'll create a List view that will iterate around a list of strings (with each string being an ingredient required for your recipe).

The next index will display a multiline Text view that will be our recipe instructions.

Finally, we'll add a `Spacer()` view at the end of our logic. The spacer will push all the content created to the top of the main view, as opposed to centering it all, which it will try and do by default:

```
} else if viewIndex == 1 {
    Text(recipe.recipe)
        .padding(15)
        .multilineTextAlignment(.leading)
}
Spacer()
```

Next, we'll set up our mock data so that we can display and work with our changes in the automatic preview canvas. The job of always creating mock data may seem like a tedious one, but this feature in SwiftUI really is a breath of fresh air and, once you've written the core of your mock data, very little maintenance will be required, although the benefits of being able to design and build with it will always be there.

Updating our mock data

With our new view all done and ready to go, you'll notice that we've added a couple of new properties to our view, so our `Helper` and `RecipeModel` struct will need updating so that we can view this in an automatic previewer. Make the following highlighted changes to the `RecipeModel.swift` file:

```
struct RecipeModel: Identifiable, Codable {
    var id = UUID()
    var name = ""
    var origin = ""
    var countryCode = ""
    var favourite = false
    var ingredients = [String]()
    var recipe = ""
}
```

As per the logic in our picker, the `ingredients` property will be a list of strings (basically a list of our ingredients) and *recipe* will be our actual recipe instructions.

Now, it's time to update our `Helper` function, so head on over to `Helper.swift` and add the following function:

```
private static func getMockIngredients() -> [String] {
    return ["1 x Ingredient One",
        "2tbp Ingredient Two",
        "500g Ingredient Three",
```

```
                    "2 x Ingredient Four"]
    }
    private static func getMockRecipe() -> String {
        return "Bacon ipsum dolor amet ad frankfurter pork aute nostrud
    leberkas jowl tenderloin dolore beef ribs. Ex tempor shankle, venison in ut
    cow deserunt. Do swine andouille, minim quis excepteur non shank eiusmod id
    buffalo. Duis shankle chuck picanha cow id minim esse. Qui burgdoggen
    capicola, venison culpa labore pastrami est minim bacon enim.\n\nExcepteur
    lorem turducken aute, qui ad hamburger chicken buffalo chislic brisket
    cupidatat pariatur. Jowl fugiat picanha pork belly quis. Ad shankle chuck
    est tri-tip ribeye sunt. Venison turkey tempor, occaecat beef biltong ut
    pork. Frankfurter sunt ad buffalo short loin cupidatat ipsum strip steak
    short ribs. Tri-tip porchetta fatback deserunt aute ut. Laborum nostrud
    aliquip pancetta deserunt, esse laboris pastrami."
    }
```

Now, there is a lot to type out here, so you may want to grab this from the sample project and simply copy and paste this in. Basically, we've created two new helper functions in order to generate some mock data. The first returns a list of strings to act as our ingredients. The second just returns a long string that acts as our recipe information. Notice that this is just using placeholder text as this data is only used to represent how the text will appear in our view.

 Lorem Ipsum, commonly used as placeholder text, is a replacement for when real text may not be available (or, in our case, 'mock data'). There are many free-to-use Lorem Ipsum generators online and some will even allow you to specify how you want the text to be generated. For the light-hearted among you, there is Bacon Ipsum, generating food-style Lorem Ipsum. Given that we are developing a recipe app, I've used Bacon Ipsum in this project.

Next, we'll need to make a couple of minor modifications to our existing mock helper functions. Make the highlighted change to each **append** in `mockRecipes()`:

```
recipies.append(RecipeModel(name: "Italian Pizza Chicken", origin: "Italy",
countryCode: "IT", ingredients: getMockIngredients(), recipe:
getMockRecipe()))
```

Going back to `RecipeDetailView.swift`, we'll need to update our `PreviewProvider` with the following logic:

```
struct RecipeDetailView_Previews: PreviewProvider {
    static var previews: some View {
        RecipeDetailView(recipe: Helper.mockRecipes().first!)
    }
}
```

Press **Resume** on the automatic preview and, with any luck, you should see your content appear in the canvas!

Now that we've seen this in the automatic preview, let's take a look at how this displays using the simulator.

Testing the new view in the simulator

Sometimes, we'll want to perform a quick test in the actual simulator rather than the automatic preview window. As we've not yet actually hooked up our view to the existing code, we won't be able to run the app in its current state and see our new View. However, we can make a small tweak with a view to performing a quick test (as long as we remember to revert it back).

Head on over to `SceneDelegate.swift` and take a look inside. `SceneDelegate` is generated as part of the project when we first create it. SwiftUI uses this to set up our views and entry points for the app. As you can see, our `ContentView` is referenced here, which is currently our main View.

To make this quick change, replace the first `ContentView` reference with the following:

```
let contentView = RecipeDetailView()
```

Then, make a quick change to the recipe model property in `RecipeDetailView.swift`:

```
//var recipe: RecipeModel!
var recipe = Helper.mockRecipes().first!
```

This is a little *hacky*, but should the automatic previewer not give you enough to test with, it's a good way to check your app in the simulator before hooking it up to the rest of your app—which is exactly what we are going to do in the next section.

App navigation

As with the majority of apps, navigation plays a massive part in how a user interacts with it—especially moving from one View to another View and, more importantly, moving back again. Navigation, or `UINavigationController` as you may have heard it referred to as, works with the concept of a navigation stack with a `RootViewController`, from where your navigation starts.

When implemented, by default, iOS will provide you with a navigation bar at the top of your screen and, in the navigation bar, you can add bar button items (such as *back*), title text, or a title view. Each time you move forward from one view to another, Navigation keeps track of this in its stack—this is often referred to as a *push*. When moving back through the stack, this is referred to as a 'pop'.

In this section, we'll incorporate navigation in our app, allowing us to select one of our recipes from our main `ContentView` and push directly to our brand new `RecipeDetailView`. We'll also update our preview provider to ensure that we can simulate the same experience in the canvas too.

We'll start by adding a `NavigationView` to the base of our app (our `ContentView.swift` file) and, from here, we'll learn how subsequent pages are called within the navigation stack.

Adding navigation to our ContentView

Head on over to `ContentView.swift`, identify the following lines of code, and then add the highlighted section:

```
var body: some View {
    NavigationView {
        VStack {
            //Existing Logic...
        }
        .navigationBarTitle(Text("My Favourite Recipes"))
    }
}
```

We'll start by wrapping a `NavigationView` around our VStack and also by adding a `navigationBarTitle` modifier to give our `NavigationView` a title.

Resume the automatic preview window to see how this looks, and you should now see your title sitting nicely above the segmented picker.

This is all well and good, but we still need to hook up each row to our new `RecipeDetailView()`. Surprisingly enough, this is done by adding one simple wrapper around our `RecipeDetailView()` iteration within our List view. Refer to the change highlighted here and make the change to your code:

```
if viewIndex == 0 {
    List(recipes, id: \.id) { recipe in
        NavigationLink(destination: RecipeDetailView(recipe: recipe)) {
```

```
                RecipeView(recipe: recipe)
            }
        }
    } else if viewIndex == 1 {
        List(Helper.getFavourites(), id: \.id) { recipe in
            NavigationLink(destination: RecipeDetailView(recipe: recipe)) {
                RecipeView(recipe: recipe)
            }
        }
    }
}
```

We simply set up a `NavigationLink` wrapper, passing in the View we want to push to, along with any required parameters (in this case, the current iteration of our `RecipeModel`) and we're done. Test run the app in the simulator by pressing *command + R*. Let's take a look at how things have panned out:

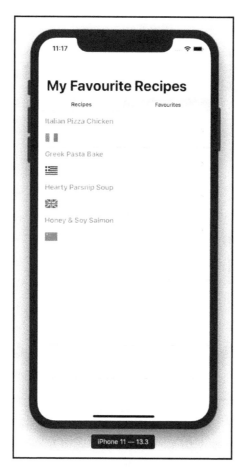

As you can see, the title of our navigation view sits nicely just above our picker. Also, each of our rows now has a disclosure indicator (like the gray arrow on the right-hand side). This is iOS's (and the `NavigationView`) way of saying that if you select this row, you'll go places... so what are you waiting for? Go and select it!:

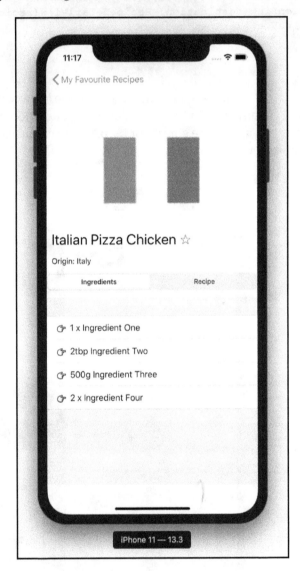

And there you have it, your `RecipeDetailView` in all its glory. Notice at the top left that your navigation bar now exists with a back chevron and that the title of your `NavigationView` looks great and even animates really well too.

Tap the back chevron to go back to `ContentView`. Now, click **Favourites** and do the same—all should be as it was with the recipe cell.

We can, however, tidy this up a little and make the interaction for the user a little more useful. Head back over to `ContentView.swift` and go back to where we implemented our `NavigationLink`. By simply adding a modifier to our `RecipeView` (within our `NavigationList`), we can control and dynamically change the title based on what segmented picker control we have selected.

Make the following highlighted changes to your existing code:

```
List(recipes, id: \.id) { recipe in
    NavigationLink(destination: RecipeDetailView(recipe: recipe)) {
        RecipeView(recipe: recipe)
            .navigationBarTitle(Text("Recipes"))
    }
}
```

We can now remove the existing `.navigationBarTitle(Text("My Favourite Recipes"))` we added earlier. Make the same change for the **Favourites** list, but change the text to "Favourites".

Run the app in the simulator and play around with it. You'll see, as you switch between each segmented picker control, that the title changes and, as you push to `RecipeDetailView`, the back button now has the corresponding title for your source View. This makes for a much-improved user experience, giving the user full knowledge of not only where they are, but where they come from and what they can expect.

In this section, we passed our model down to `RecipeDetailView` in order for our view to consume the data. In the next section, we'll look at how we can use `@EnvironmentObject` to use a single property throughout all of our Views.

Accessing with @EnvironmentObject

Previously passing objects between views (or more specifically `ViewControllers`) could get a bit tricky, whilst the delegate pattern was a solid tried and tested method, passing data backup through multiple layers could get a little repetitive and in some cases complicated.

However with SwiftUI, and the use of `EnvironmentObject`, we don't need to worry about that anymore, as we'll learn in this next section we can take an object at the very top of our hierarchy and use this as deep as we need to within our Views; it's a global object which is accessible everywhere.

Adding and injecting the @EnvironmentObject class

To begin with, we'll need to create a class that can conform to the `ObservableObject` protocol, as it's only going to contain one property. For now, we'll just create this at the bottom of our `ContentView.swift` file.

Go ahead and add the following code:

```
class AppData: ObservableObject {
    @Published var fontColor = Color.black
}
```

We've created a class called `AppData`. During the course of this book, we'll add various other properties that we'll want our SwiftUI Views to access on a more global scale. We'll start by adding a `fontColor` variable, which will allow us to set the color of our fonts in one place, but be accessible in another.

We create our variable called `fontColor` and prefix this with `@Published`.

Now that we've got that set up, let's head on over to the `SceneDelegate.swift` file and add the following highlighted code:

```
let appData = AppData()

let contentView = ContentView()

// Use a UIHostingController as window root view controller.
if let windowScene = scene as? UIWindowScene {
...
```

Here, we are creating an instance of our new `AppData()` class, which we'll now use to inject into our `ContentView` (as our `ContentView` is the root view of our entire app's view hierarchy).

Make the change highlighted here in order to inject `AppData()` into our `ContentView`:

```
let window = UIWindow(windowScene: windowScene)
window.rootViewController = UIHostingController(rootView:
contentView.environmentObject(appData))
```

We've now successfully set up our environment object. In the next part, we'll cover how we can use this within our app.

Using @EnvironmentObject

Once we've set up our environment object, we can now declare and use our `UserData` class from any View we like. Let's try it out. Head on over to `RecipeDetailView.swift` and add the following:

```
@EnvironmentObject var appData: AppData
```

Notice that we are not initializing any data here or being forced to set this as forced or as optional. That is because we've already injected the data into our View hierarchy back in `SceneDelegate.swift`.

 Regardless of whether you've injected the data or not, you can still declare an `@EnvironmentObject` in your project. However, if there is no data injected and your app references it, it will crash.

Let's try this out now. Still in `RecipeDetailView.swift`, make the following highlighted change in order to reference your `setting.fontColor` value:

```
Text("\(recipe.name)")
    .font(.title)
    .padding(.leading, 10)
    .foregroundColor(self.settings.fontColor)
// Favourites Button
Button(action: {
    Helper.addRemoveFavourite(recipe: self.recipe)
    self.settings.fontColor = self.isFavourite ? .orange : .black
    self.recipe.favourite.toggle()
}) {
    Image(systemName: isFavourite ? "star.fill" : "star")
}
```

In order to demonstrate how this works, when our `Favourites` button is clicked, we check the current value of `isFavorite` and assign either `.orange` or `.blue` to our global `AppData().fontColor)` environment variable.

Go ahead and run the app and try it out for yourself. You'll see that by clicking the Favorite star, your Text View automatically updates its color to orange. Now, you're probably thinking, why is that so different from using the `@State` variable and setting the desired color?

Well, head on over to `RecipeView.swift` and add in a reference to our environment variable, just like we did in `RecipeDetailView.swift`:

```
@EnvironmentObject var appData: AppData
```

Then, make the following highlighted change:

```
Text("\(recipe.name)")
    .font(.headline)
    .foregroundColor(appData.fontColor)
    .bold()
```

Now rerun your test by going into a recipe, selecting this as a favorite, and then, when you head back to the list of recipes, you'll see that the font color for all the items has been updated to orange.

Let's now take this a step further and really harness the power of `@EnvironmentObject`.

Using EnvironmentObject as a single source of truth

The beauty of using `@EnvironmentObject` is that in certain cases, we can use properties or objects within its class as a single source of truth. By this, I mean that we don't have to worry about passing around different copies of objects and data or worry about constantly reading or writing data from our persistence store (as we're currently doing for favorites in `UserDefaults`).

Let's start by extending our `AppData()` class to include an array of our `RecipeModel()`. Make the following highlighted changes:

```
class AppData: ObservableObject {
    @Published var fontColor = Color.black
    @Published var recipes = [RecipeModel]()
    var favourites: [RecipeModel] {
```

```
        return recipes.filter({ $0.favourite == true })
    }

    func updateRecipe(recipe: RecipeModel) {
        recipes = recipes.filter( { $0.id != recipe.id } )
        recipes.append(recipe)
    }

}
```

Here, we've added a @Published variable for our array of RecipeModel() and we've also created another computed property for our favorites, which basically reads from our recipes variable and performs a filter to only include those that have a value of favorite == true.

Another function that we've added is an updateRecipe() function, which we'll use a little later on.

Next, we need to update our SceneDelegate.swift file in order to read our mock data into our environment object when the app first launches. Make the following highlighted change:

```
let appData = AppData()
appData.recipes = Helper.mockRecipes()
```

Now, head back on over to ContentView.swift and let's add a reference to our @EnvironmentObject:

```
@EnvironmentObject var appData: AppData
```

With all that done, make the following changes to our List Views so that we can read the content from our @EnvironmentObject:

```
if viewIndex == 0 {
    List(appData.recipes, id: \.id) { recipe in
        NavigationLink(destination: RecipeDetailView(recipe: recipe)) {
            RecipeView(recipe: recipe)
                .navigationBarTitle(Text("Recipes"))
        }
    }
} else if viewIndex == 1 {
    List(appData.favourites, id: \.id) { recipe in
        NavigationLink(destination: RecipeDetailView(recipe: recipe)) {
            RecipeView(recipe: recipe)
                .navigationBarTitle(Text("Favourites"))
        }
```

```
        }
    }
```

Now that we are reading data from our recipe list, which is not only a single source of truth, but is available to us throughout our app at any given time. Let's make an amendment to our `RecipeDetailView.swift` and see exactly how this is done.

Make the following highlighted changes to the click action on our favorites button:

```
// Favourites Button
Button(action: {
    self.settings.fontColor = self.isFavourite ? .orange : .black
    self.recipe.favourite.toggle()
    self.appData.updateRecipe(recipe: self.recipe)
}) {
    Image(systemName: isFavourite ? "star.fill" : "star")
}
```

Here, we've added a call to our `updateRecipe` function that lives within our `@EnvironmentObject`, passing in our newly modified recipe (notice how we've only added this once we have performed the `.toggle()`). The call to this function now replaces the need to persist the favorites data—we just need to persist an array or `RecipeModel()` instead, but as we are not yet adding any new recipes to our list and still reading from our mock data, we'll look at doing that in the next chapter.

EnvironmentObject best practices

So far, we've learned what `@EnvironmentObject` has to offer and we have to admit that it's pretty powerful, but as with most things in software development, we need to be careful not to over-engineer our solution just because something is easy to do.

It's very tempting to simply use `@EnvironmentObject` to store all data passed between views; we could even store a dictionary in there with a key to match our view name and a value to hold some values.

However, those of you who are familiar with the singleton pattern will know all too well that this approach can soon become messy and far too complicated than it needs to be.

When choosing to use `@EnvironmentObject`, don't think about why you want to use it, but more why you need to use it.

Take our example as a good base. Passing and updating the array of `RecipeModel` back and forth is heavy lifting and serves no real purpose as we only need to persist to it when we add a new recipe or update the favorite status. Going from our `ContentView()` to our `RecipeDetailView()`, we simply pass the `RecipeModel()` across in the constructor, so our recipe variable is ready and available for us to use:

```
NavigationLink(destination: RecipeDetailView(recipe: recipe))
```

More often than not, you'll be using a navigation controller or a modal to present a new View, so the option to use a constructor will always be there. The added bonus of this, as we've seen in previous chapters, is that we can inject mock data straight into our views without the need for mocking up an `@EnvironmentObject`.

With that in mind, there is always the odd occasion when we do need to send mock data via our `@EnvironmentObject`, so let's take a look at how we would achieve that.

Mock EnvironmentObject

With the above in place, we're really starting to build a good solid architecture for our app, but now that we have made use of `@EnvironmentObject`, we need to make some minor adjustments to our `PreviewProvider` in order to inject in our own mock environment.

We'll first need to create an instance of our `@EnvironmentObject AppData()` class within our preview struct:

```
struct ContentView_Previews: PreviewProvider {
    static let appData = AppData()
    static var previews: some View {
        ContentView().environmentObject(appData)
    }
}
```

Next, we'll need to add some mock data to the new instance:

```
struct ContentView_Previews: PreviewProvider {
    static let appData = AppData()
    static var previews: some View {
        appData.recipes = Helper.mockRecipes()
        return ContentView().environmentObject(appData)
    }
}
```

All we've done here is assign the `recipes` variable to read in our mock data. Notice how we've had to add a return statement to our `ContentView()` line so that SwiftUI knows exactly what View we want to return (as basically, we've added some non-view code in there).

Another added bonus, given that `@EnvironmentObject` also conforms to `@Observable`, is that should the object change (or get updated), our changes disappear too. Try it out, run the app in the simulator, mark some recipes as favorites, and then revisit the recipe again to see that the value has been persisted.

In this section, we covered how to create a global data object that can be used throughout our app, we covered how to initialize the object within our `SceneDelegate`, and then demonstrated how it can be referenced and, more importantly, used in any of our new or existing Views.

Summary

In this chapter, we took the basic structure of our app to the next level. We started by creating another View, which took data that we selected from a list in our previous view. We looked at how we can reuse our mock data to make working on the preview provider a much easier (and more beneficial experience).

Next, we introduced ourselves to navigation and how the navigation stack works within mobile apps. We hooked up our new and existing Views, which allowed us to interact between the two.

Finally, we learned how to use `EnvironmentObject` to inject and give us a global object that can be used anywhere in our app. We then modified our logic to make use of our new environment, reducing the need for us to use our previously written logic.

In our next chapter, we'll create another View that we'll use to create and add our own recipe. We'll integrate this directly into our app's navigation stack and make further use of our recently created `EnvironmentObject` logic.

Questions

1. What View do we add in order to push content to the top of our current View?
2. In a navigation hierarchy, what is the first View known as?
3. What modifier do we use to add a title to our `NavigationView`?
4. What do we need to wrap our list content in, in order to push to a destination View?
5. What must we make sure that we do in order to prevent a crash when we use an `@EnvironmentObject` property?

Further reading

- **Lorum Ipsum:** `https://en.wikipedia.org/wiki/Lorem_ipsum`
- **SwiftUI Navigation View:** `https://developer.apple.com/documentation/swiftui/navigationview`
- **SwiftUI Environment Object**: `https://developer.apple.com/documentation/swiftui/environmentobject`

7
Creating a Form with States and Data Binding

In this chapter, we're going to create a brand-new View that allows us to add our own recipe to our app. We'll create multiple input forms along with a dynamic list as we add ingredients to our recipe. In the header, we'll add a placeholder image that we can overwrite by choosing a photo from our library. Included in our form will be a picker much like the segmented picker we created earlier but using the more default look and feel that we are used to from a picker in iOS.

Once we've created our form, we'll save all the data so it can be referenced and favorited in our app, just like our mock data.

The following topics will be covered in this chapter:

- Creating our recipe form View
- Adding images from our library
- Adding a multiline text input and country picker
- Persisting our recipe

Technical requirements

For this chapter, you'll need to download Xcode version 11.3 or above from the Apple Mac App Store. You'll also need to be running the latest version of macOS (Catalina or above).

Simply search for Xcode in the App Store and select and download the latest version.

Launch Xcode and follow any additional installation instructions that your system may prompt you with. Once Xcode has fully launched, you're ready to go.

Creating our recipe form View

In this section, we'll start the beginning of our form. There are multiple ways we could tackle this, either by creating a VStack and a list of Views or by creating our own custom View and iterating through a `ListView` of options.

But in the case of our app, I'll introduce you to forms and sections. Other than the obvious naming of the controls, forms do a great job of making our desired layout really simple and with very little effort.

Let's start by adding a couple of text fields to visualize how this all looks.

Implementing text and text fields

We'll start by creating a new SwiftUI View. We'll create a new file in our Xcode project called `RecipeDetailView` by highlighting the group name in the File Tree, then right-clicking and selecting **New File**. Select **SwiftUI View** from the **User Interface** options and click **Next**. Call your new file `AddRecipeView.swift` and click **Create.**

Next, we're going to add some text fields to our main View that will allow us to input text for our recipe name and ingredients. There are a couple of ways we could approach this, but the simplest way would be to make use of the form View in SwiftUI. Let's add a couple of forms and see how this looks:

```
Form {
    Section(header: Text("Add Recipe Name:")) {
        TextField("enter recipe name", text: $recipeName)
    }
    Section(header: Text("Add Ingredient:")) {
        TextField("enter ingredient name", text: $ingredient)
    }
}
```

We start by adding a `Form` wrapper in the body of our app; from here we've added two *Section* wrappers each taking a parameter of `header`—the header allows us to add a Text View where we can set a name for each section we create.

Inside each section, we add a `TextField`, with a placeholder name first and a property for the text that is being entered. As you can see, we're referencing two `@State` variables so that we can bind and monitor the change we make here. Let's go ahead and add those before we go any further:

```
@State internal var recipeName: String = ""
@State internal var ingredient: String = ""
@State internal var ingredients = [String]()
```

Remember to add the preceding code just inside our struct, but outside of our body.

Now we've got these added, let's take a look at them on the automatic preview canvas if not already loaded—click **Resume** and you should see the following:

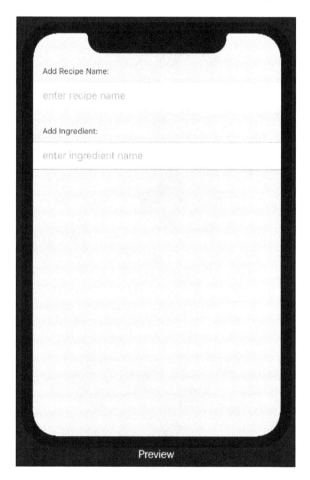

Now, let's go a bit deeper. Remember from the previous chapter how we used mock data to inject an array of ingredients? We'll need to create a UI in order to build up the ingredients list in the same way. A nice way to go about this would be by adding a plus button at the end of the `TextField`—this would allow us to not only add each ingredient to an array but to also validate that there is actually something there.

Out of the box, SwiftUI doesn't currently have anything in terms of modifiers that suits our needs for this, but that doesn't mean we can't be creative. Let's take a look at how we can create our own custom modifier to achieve this.

Creating our first custom modifier

For this, we'll need to define another struct. We can do this in the same file as `AddRecipeView.swift`, but just directly below our main struct. Start by adding the following snippet, and we'll go through it line by line:

```
struct AddButton: ViewModifier {
    @Binding var text: String
    @Binding var ingredients: [String]
    public func body(content: Content) -> some View {
        ZStack(alignment: .trailing) {
            content
            Button(action: {
                if self.text != "" {
                    self.ingredients.append(self.text)
                    self.text = ""
                }
            }) {
                Image(systemName: "plus")
                    .foregroundColor(Color(UIColor.opaqueSeparator))
            }
            .padding(.trailing, 8)
        }
    }
}
```

We'll start with the declaration; we create a new struct called `AddButton` that extends from the `ViewModifier` protocol. As all objects in SwifUI are Views, we don't need to specify what type of View this is going to be used for (that is, `Button`, `TextField`, `Picker`, and so on):

struct AddButton: ViewModifier

Next, we create a couple of variables. Note that we've prefixed these with @Binding. That's because the values being passed in will be @State values so we want to enable two-way binding:

```
@Binding var text: String
@Binding var ingredients: [String]
```

From this, we'll create our body. This is much like when we work with body in our main Views, although there is one slight difference. Can you see it, and do you know why:

```
public func body(content: Content) -> some View
```

That's right, we pass in the content of the View that the modifier we are building is being used for. We'll need to reference this content inside our modifier in order for the View to render correctly (or basically, our modifier will show minus the actual View we originally rendered).

Now, let's add some more logic inside our body:

```
ZStack(alignment: .trailing) {
    content
    Button(action: {
        if self.text != "" {
            self.ingredients.append(self.text)
            self.text = ""
        }
    }) {
        Image(systemName: "plus")
            .foregroundColor(Color(UIColor.opaqueSeparator))
        }
        .padding(.trailing, 8)
}
```

Here, we are being introduced to a ZStack. Similar to an HStack and VStack, ZStack allows content to be added either in front or stacked on top of each other, as opposed to stacking horizontally or vertically. With this in mind, we can still set an alignment parameter—in this case, we've set .trailing.

As previously mentioned, we'll still need to include the parent View's content followed by any other Views or logic we require for our modifier—in this case, we've added a button.

Our button, when clicked, does two things. First, it checks to see if the text passed in is empty—if not, then it proceeds to add this to our `Ingredients` array, which we too passed in. As our `Ingredients` array has a two-way binding to the property declared from our parent struct, this will force SwiftUI to update the current state, hereby allowing us to make use of the `Ingredients` array with the newly added value should we wish to do so (which we will shortly).

We've again made use of SF Symbols and added a system image named `"plus"` that will be displayed when our modifier is added. Now that we've got our modifier all written up, let's hook it up to our `TextField` and see what it looks like:

```
Section(header: Text("Add Ingredient:")) {
    TextField("enter ingredient name", text: $ingredient)
        .modifier(AddButton(text: $ingredient, ingredients: $ingredients))
}
```

We've simply added our modifier to our `TextField`, creating a new instance of `AddButton` and passing across the two `@State` variables we created earlier. If it's not already updated, press **Resume** on the automatic preview window and you should see the following changes:

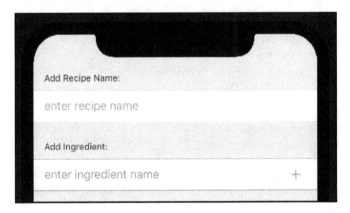

As you can see, we have a nice plus button at the end of our `TextField`. We can update the Preview Provider to inject some dummy data, but at this point, we'll only see the recipe name `TextField` populated. In order to test the *Add* functionality, we'll need to launch the simulator, but again we don't really do anything once we add the data so there's not going to be much to show. Let's change that and create a list based on the ingredients we add.

Back in our main body, add the following code beneath our last section:

```
if ingredients.count > 0 {
    Section(header: Text("Current Ingredients:")) {
        List(ingredients, id: \.self) { item in
            Button(action: {
                self.ingredients.removeAll { $0 == item }
            }) {
            Image(systemName: "minus")
                .foregroundColor(Color(UIColor.opaqueSeparator))
            }
            .padding(.trailing, 8)
            Text(item)
        }
    }
}
```

Here, we have created a `Section` with the title `"Current Ingredients"`. This will iterate around our `@State` variable, `ingredients`, and add them to a list. Note that we've added a button here that, when pressed, removes the items from our list—again, as this is held together by a two-way binding, SwiftUI takes care of reloading our View and our list will be updated automatically.

We've also added a little safeguard in too. If our array of ingredients is empty and has no content, we won't show the section header (as that won't look right).

Now that we've got something to show, let's update our `PreviewProvider` so we can see the changes in the automatic preview canvas:

```
struct AddRecipeView_Previews: PreviewProvider {
    static var previews: some View {
        let recipe = Helper.mockRecipes().first!
        return AddRecipeView(recipeName: recipe.name, ingredient:
recipe.ingredients.first!, ingredients: recipe.ingredients)
    }
}
```

Update the Preview Provider with the highlighted code. As you can see, we once again use the `mockRecipe()` helper function to grab the first recipe out of the array.

In `Chapter 1`, *Getting Started with SwiftUI*, we talked about force unwrapping and how it should be avoided unless absolutely necessary. In the previous snippet, we use force unwrapping to grab the first recipe from our helper as it is not directly in our production code (and for the simplicity of this book). This is one of the occasions where it's okay to do this—but don't get into any bad habits!

If you have not already, press **Resume** in the automatic preview canvas, and you should see the following:

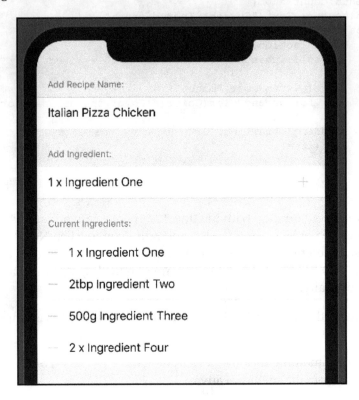

Perfect! We're making some really good progress with our app now, but before we build any more components, let's hook this page up and test it in the simulator.

Adding a button to the navigation bar

Now that we've got our navigation bar all set up, let's look at how we add a button to it.

First of all, let's head back over to `ContentView.swift`. We're going to add a modifier called `navigationBarButtonItems`—for those who have worked with `UINavigation` controls previously, this will suddenly feel like familiar territory. Adding a navigation bar button item to your Navigation View allows you to add Views (anything from images, to text, to buttons) to the top navigation bar in your app.

Although not set in stone, adding a button that presents another View often leads to a View being presented modally as opposed to being added and pushed along the Navigation Views stack. Let's implement the following just beneath the end of our VStack and see what effect we get:

```
.navigationBarItems(trailing:
    Button(action: {
        self.showAddRecipe.toggle()
    }) {
    Image(systemName: "plus")
        .renderingMode(.original)
    }.sheet(isPresented: $showAddRecipe) {
        AddRecipeView().environmentObject(self.appData)
    }
)
```

Going through the preceding code, you can see we've added a modifier that takes a parameter, trailing, which in turn accepts any Views we want to add. In this case, we've added an image with an SF Symbol called plus, which toggles a @State variable Boolean called showAddRecipe (which you'll need to declare).

A further modifier is added called .sheet, which will present a modal based on the state of the isPresented parameter. Any View inside the .sheet modifier will be displayed in the modal (in this case AddRecipeView()). Note here that we've passed in @EnvironmentObject—this is because we're changing navigation stacks slightly, from a segue in the current stack to a modal being presented.

If it's not already updated, press **Resume** on the automatic preview canvas, and you should now see a plus symbol in the top-right corner of the navigation controller.

Now, let's fire this all up in the iOS simulator and see all our good work in action. If all has gone well, you should be able to press the *plus* button to present our new View and, using the controls we created, add ingredients to our View, which will dynamically update our new **Current Ingredients** list in our app.

In this section, we learned how to use forms and sections in order to create a more user-friendly input view. We created our first modifier, which not only allowed us to create custom functionality for our TextField but showed off more of how two-way binding is used in SwiftUI.

Adding in a bit of a hack

Now, you'll see me mention a couple of times during this book that SwiftUI is still in its infancy. At the time of writing this book, there was a known issue that when you tap on a `NavigationBarItem` in order to present a sheet (just like we are doing with our `AddRecipeView`), should you try to tap on the same button again (once said sheet is dismissed) without performing any other interaction, the button would simply be unclickable.

A temporary workaround discovered by the Apple community is to add the following highlighted code just before we create our `NavigationBarItem`:

```
.navigationBarTitle(Text(""), displayMode: .inline) // Hack due to bug in
Xcode!
.navigationBarItems(trailing:
    Button(action: {
        self.showAddRecipe.toggle()
    }) { ...
```

This does have a slight knock-on effect with our `.navigationBarTitle` , so, going forward, we'll need to remove these from `ContentView()`:

```
.navigationBarTitle(Text("Favourites"))
.navigationBarTitle(Text("Recipes"))
```

With that done, everything should work as expected and, hopefully, by the time you're reading this book, Apple will be well on their way to fixing it!

In the next section, we'll create a View where we can capture an image directly from our photo library and add it to our recipe.

Adding images from our library

For this section, we're going to use some boilerplate code in order to get our app to select images directly from our camera library (or camera roll as some may refer to it) and insert them into our app. While this is a useful way to integrate image lookup from within SwiftUI, it is a little advanced and out of scope for this book.

First of all, make sure you've downloaded the source code for this chapter. Once you've got this, you're looking for a file called `ImageHelper.swift`. Simply drag the file from Finder into your File Tree (place it just under your existing `Helper.swift` file).

The file we've added is a helper. It accesses the photo library and returns an image that has been selected by the user. We'll see shortly how that all hooks up.

 If you are interested in how we achieve this, take a look at the links in the *Further reading* section.

Now that file is in, do a quick *command + B* to make sure everything builds okay—with all that done, let's add an image to our app.

Creating our Image View

Back over in our `AddReciepeView.swift` file, add the following highlighted `@State` variables underneath our existing ones:

```
@State internal var ingredients = [String]()
@State internal var showingImagePicker = false
@State private var libraryImage: UIImage?
```

Now, add the following highlighted code just inside the start of your form (above the *Add Recipe Name Text View*):

```
Form {
    Image(uiImage: self.libraryImage ?? (UIImage(named: "placeholder-add-
image") ?? UIImage()))
        .resizable()
        .aspectRatio(contentMode: .fit)
        .clipShape(Circle())
        .overlay(Circle().stroke(Color.purple, lineWidth: 3).shadow(radius:
10))
        .frame(maxWidth: .infinity, maxHeight: 230)
        .padding(6)
```

So, going line by line we've started by adding an Image View into our VStack, which is asking for a UIImage to be passed in—for the moment, we'll reference the libraryImage variable we just created. As libraryImage is optional we'll have to provide a default value—that works perfectly for us because we'll simply provide a placeholder image called placeholder-add-image. This might start to look a little messy now because creating a UIImage from a name returns an optional type too, so again we have to provide a default value of UIImage(). This happens because the compiler doesn't know if the image corresponding to the name we provided will always be available.

 We're creating our Image View with a UIImage because our previously imported ImageHelper returns the type of UIImage(). UIImage is UIKit's version of SwiftUI's Image.

Next, we'll decorate our Image View with some modifiers. We'll start by adding .resizeable() and aspectRatio(contentMode: .fit). These will allow our image to fit perfectly into the frame of our Image View. It may cause some slight cropping, but as you'll see next we are going to border our Image View with a circle, so that doesn't really matter.

We'll now add the following modifiers to give your ImageView a nice circle effect, set the height of our View, and add some padding:

```
.clipShape(Circle())
.overlay(Circle().stroke(Color.purple, lineWidth: 3).shadow(radius: 10))
.frame(maxWidth: .infinity, maxHeight: 230)
.padding(6)
```

As you can see from the overlay modifier, we add a Circle() View with a stroke width of 3 and set the color to purple—we then add a shadow to this with a radius of 10.

If it's not already updated, press **Resume** on the automatic preview canvas and we should see our changes. Notice anything missing? That's right, our placeholder image is missing! You'll need to grab it from the downloaded source code and add it to the Assets.xcassets catalog (remembering to give it the same name as we set previously, **placeholder-add-image**). Press **Resume** again and all should be well!

Implementing our ImageHelper

Now, let's hook up a button that we'll use to call and select our images from our library. For simplicity, we'll amend our previously created Image View to be a `Button` (with our image inside). Amend the following `Image` code to wrap this within a button control:

```
Button(action: {
    self.showingImagePicker.toggle()
}) {
    Image(uiImage: self.libraryImage ?? (UIImage(named: "placeholder-add-
image") ?? UIImage()))
        .resizable()
        .aspectRatio(contentMode: .fit)
        .clipShape(Circle())
        .overlay(Circle().stroke(Color.purple, lineWidth: 3).shadow(radius:
10))
        .frame(maxWidth: .infinity, maxHeight: 230)
        .padding(6)
}
.sheet(isPresented: $showingImagePicker) {
    ImagePicker(image: self.$libraryImage)
}.buttonStyle(PlainButtonStyle())
```

Let's go through the code one step at a time:

1. First, we add a `Button` View that, when used, toggles the Boolean value of `showingImagePicker`, which we set previously. As `showingImagePicker` is a `@State` variable, SwiftUI will reload the layout once this value has been changed (which you'll see the effect of shortly).

2. Next, we'll copy in the Image View content that we previously created.

3. Now, we'll add a `sheet` modifier similar to the one we created when initially calling the `AddReciepeView.swift` file. We'll pass in the `showingImagePicker` variable to determine if this sheet is to be presented or not when the view is loaded (which is why we `toggle()` the value in the action). When our AddRecipeView sheet is shown, we'll invoke the `ImagePicker()` function (which lives inside our `ImageHelper`) passing in the `libraryImage` state variable we declared earlier.

   Again, using the power of states in SwiftUI, once we've selected an image, our `libraryImage` variable will be updated by the `ImagePicker` and again our View will be reloaded—this time showing the image selected.

4. Finally, we'll need to add the `buttonStyle` modifier to our button and set it to `PlainButtonStyle()`. This is required in order to render our image within our Button View correctly.

5. If it's not already updated, press **Resume** on the automatic preview canvas and we should see our changes. It should look something like this:

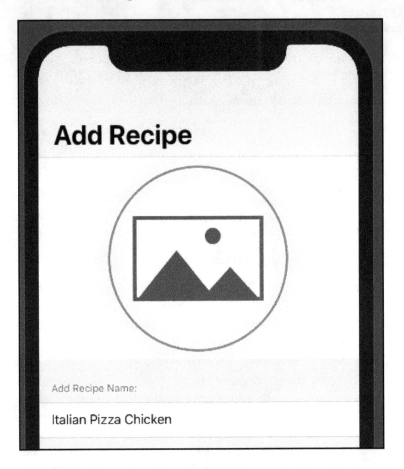

Now that we've got that looking all well and good, fire up the simulator by pressing *command + R* and try it out for yourself. The iOS simulator comes with some pre-loaded image for you to have a play with... looks good, right?

In this section, we added an Image View that doubles up as a button that allows us to select a photo from our library and use it for our recipe. We covered some more modifiers in order to make the presentation of our Image View a little less basic. We also saw how we can tap into exciting Swift functions and perform a callback to the parent View in order to power our SwiftUI frontend (such as our `ImageHelper`).

In the next section, we'll touch again on using UIKit to help us create a multiline Text View where we can add instructions to add to our recipe.

Adding a multiline text input and country picker

At the time of writing this book, there is no native way of creating a multiline Text View using only SwiftUI components. In order to achieve this, we'll have to tap into our old friend UIKit. Much like the helper we created in the previous section, we'll basically create a wrapper around `UITextView` (which in turn allows multiline support) and bring it back as a SwiftUI View.

As previously mentioned, this is a little out of scope for this book, but in a later chapter, we'll cover this in a little more detail for those of you who are familiar with UIKit's exciting components and are interested in using them.

Implementing a UITextView wrapper

First of all, we need to start by creating a wrapper for our UITextView.

Head on over to the source code you downloaded earlier and grab a file called `TextHelper.swift`. Drag it into your current project via the File Tree (again, add this under your existing Helpers).

Once you've added this in, do a quick *command + B* to make sure everything is happy.

Now, head back over to `AddRecipeView.swift` and we're going to add another `@State` variable. Add the following highlighted code:

```
@State internal var ingredients = [String]()
@State internal var recipeDetails: String = ""
```

Then, locate where we last added a **section**, because we are going to add a new section for our recipe details. Add the following code:

```
Section(header: Text("Details")) {
    TextView(text: $recipeDetails)
        .frame(height: 220)
}
```

If it's not already updated, press **Resume** on the automatic preview canvas and we should see our changes.

Looking good! Our form is coming on in leaps and bounds now. Use *command + R* run this in the simulator to see how you can now input multiple lines.

Next, let's update our `PreviewProvider` to add some dummy data. Make the following highlighted change and press **Resume** on the automatic preview canvas:

```
struct AddRecipeView_Previews: PreviewProvider {
    static var previews: some View {
        let recipe = Helper.mockRecipes().first!
        return AddRecipeView(recipeName: recipe.name, ingredient:
recipe.ingredients.first ?? "", ingredients: recipe.ingredients,
recipeDetails: recipe.recipe)
    }
}
```

Now we are using a Navigation View. Let's add a navigation title in order to really finish off our form. Add the following modifier just after our closing form brace:

```
    } // Closing Form Brace
    .navigationBarTitle("Add Recipe")
}
```

Fire up the simulator again and have a play. It should all be coming together just nicely now, both programmatically and visually.

You should see something like the following:

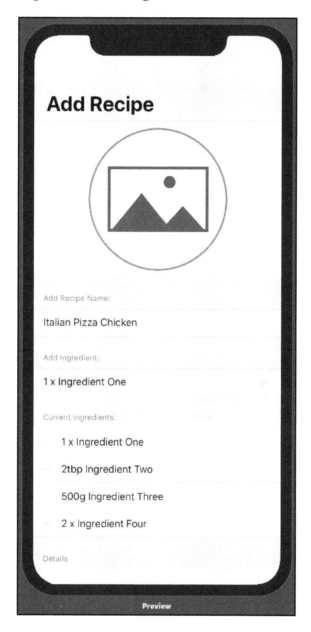

Our preview canvas should be looking great now, full of dummy data for us to test and work with. Now let's add our final field—a country picker.

Adding a country picker

Within our mock data, we've been using a predefined country to look up our flag images. We'll also use this later on in the project too, making it a mandatory field that we'll need to add to our `AddRecipeView`.

First, we'll start by creating some mock data. Head on over to `Helper.swift` and create the following helper function:

```
static func getCountries() -> [String] {
    return ["Italy", "Greece", "UK", "China", "France", "USA", "Mexico",
"Spain"]
}
```

For the purpose of this book, I've only added a few random countries, but you can add as many as you want. Next, head over to `AddRecipeView.swift` and create another `Section()`. This time called it `"Country of Origin:"`:

```
Section(header: Text("Country of Origin:")) {
}
```

Next, we'll add a picker. This time, we'll use a default picker that, when tapped from our form, will push us to a list of countries to select. Make the following highlighted changes to your new `Section()`:

```
Section(header: Text("Country of Origin:")) {
    Picker(selection: $selectedCountry, label: Text("Country")) {
        ForEach(0 ..< countries.count) {
            Text(self.countries[$0]).tag($0)
        }
    }
}
```

Much like our other picker, we're required to have a @State variable to keep track of what has been selected. Also, if you look at the preceding code, you'll see that we are iterating around an array called countries. This is mock data we've taken from the helper function we just created. Let's add these declarations now at the top of our file:

```
@State private var selectedCountry = 0
internal var countries = Helper.getCountries()
```

Now, back to the picker. Note inside the iteration that we create a Text View for each value. This basically generates the list we'll see for the country names in our array. Let's *command + R* and check this out in the simulator.

So, all going well, the picker should be displayed, but the only problem is that when we click on it, nothing happens.

This is because the picker we've used requires us to perform a push to another View, as we're no longer in our Navigation View (as we presented AddReciepeView via a modal)—we've nowhere to push this to.

We can fix this by simply wrapping our form inside a Navigation View like so:

```
NavigationView {
    Form {
        Button(action: {
            self.showingImagePicker.toggle()
            .
            .
            .
    } // Closing Form Brace
    .navigationBarTitle("Add Recipe")
}
```

Run the simulator and try again. All going well, you should now be pushed to a list just like the following:

In this section, we added a multiline Text View with the aid of our old friends UIKit and UITextView, and from this learned that it's still okay to keep up to date with advancements in these frameworks as we wait for SwiftUI to mature and develop further. We also revisited using a Picker View, but this time using its default behavior as opposed to a `SegmentedControl`. We learned how this can fit nicely within a form; however, using it in this state does require us to be in the Navigation View stack.

In the next section, we'll look at persisting our recipe model so that we can add these to our main lists and favorites. We'll cover how to take the image we've supplied and convert it to data to store in our app. We'll also cover how to dismiss the modal we've created once we are done with it without the need for any user interaction.

Persisting our recipe

In this section, we'll bundle up all the data we've received from our form and persist it down to our app so we can save the recipe and later view it via our main list or favorites. First, we'll look at how to convert the image we've taken into data so that we can successfully persist it to our `UserDefaults` and retrieve it again when necessary. We'll also cover how to use a fallback image if there is a problem accessing the image we've saved.

Once we've covered that, we'll use a helper function similar to the one we used for our favorites to both retrieve and save our recipe.

Persisting our image

First off, we'll need to make some tweaks to our `RecipeModel()`. Head on over to the `RecipeModel.swift` file and make the following highlighted changes:

```
var ingredients = [String]()
var recipe = ""
var imageData: Data?
var image: UIImage {
    if let dataImage = UIImage(data: imageData ?? Data()) {
        return dataImage
    } else if let countryImage = UIImage(named: countryCode) {
        return countryImage
    }
    return UIImage()
}
```

Here, we've added one property called `imageData` and a computed property called `image`.

The `imageData` property will be home to the converted `UIImage` that we previously selected. Converting the image to `Data()` will allow this to be successfully persisted to `UserDefaults`.

Our computed property doesn't hold value as such; it simply returns a type (in this case, `UIImage`) based on conditions of other properties in our model. In this case, if we can successfully convert the `imageData` property to a `UIImage()` it will return that—if that fails, it will attempt to create an image from the `countryCode` (like we originally had), before finally just returning an empty instance of `UIImage()` (a blank image, basically).

With this change made, we'll now need to make a couple of changes through our app. First head on over to `RecipeView.swift` and make the following highlighted changes to where we added our original flag image:

```
Text ("\(recipe.name)")
    .font(.headline)
    .foregroundColor(Color.blue)
    .bold()
Image(uiImage: recipe.image).resizable()
  .aspectRatio(contentMode: .fit)
  .frame(height: 30)
```

Here, we're changing our Image View to accept a `UIImage` from our `RecipeModel()` and resize it according to how we want it to display. If we don't do this, our Image View will respect the original size and will be imported more than likely filling the entire screen.

Next, head on over to our `RecipeDetailView.swift` file and make a similar highlighted change:

```
var body: some View {
    // VStack so we can list our components vertically
    VStack(alignment: .leading, spacing: 15) {
    // Image (currently using flag)
    Image(uiImage: recipe.image)
        .resizable()
        .aspectRatio(contentMode: .fit)
        .frame(maxWidth: .infinity, maxHeight: 200)
```

Again, we are modifying our Image View to accept the image property we created in our `RecipeModel()`, also adding a couple of modifiers to adjust the size accordingly too.

Now, we need to grab the image we've brought in and converted it to a `Data()` type in order for us to be able to persist it with `UserDefault`. Back over in `AddRecipeView.swift`, create the following private function:

```
private func saveRecipe() {
    var recipeImage = UIImage()
    if let libImage = libraryImage {
        recipeImage = libImage
    }
    let newRecipe = RecipeModel(id: UUID(),
                                name: recipeName,
                                origin: countries[selectedCountry],
                                countryCode:
Helper.getCountryCode(country: country),
                                favourite: false,
                                ingredients: ingredients,
                                recipe: recipeDetails,
                                imageData:
recipeImage.jpegData(compressionQuality: 0.3) ?? Data())
    appData.recipes.append(newRecipe)
    Helper.saveRecipes(recipe: appData.recipes)
}
```

Going through the preceding code, we'll first perform a safeguarding check on the `libraryImage` property (as you'll remember, this was an optional type). Once we're happy and have reassigned it to a local variable called `recipeImage`, we can now continue to build up our model.

We'll start by creating a new instance of `RecipeModel()`, but we'll now begin to build this up by adding the values we've got in the constructor. I've separated out each line in the preceding code to show you the parameters and variables you'll need to pass in. If you take a closer look at the `imageData` parameter, you'll notice that we've added the `.jpegData()` function to our `recipeImage` variable. This is a function available in Swift that will nicely convert a `UIImage` to a JPG data type, ready for us to persist.

You'll also notice a call to a `Helper()` function called `getCountryCode()`, which accepts a parameter of `country`. This is a simple lookup to get the country code from the country name we chose in order to select our image later on. It's a basic switch statement, so nothing too exciting to go over—pop over to the same code and copy and paste it into your project.

Persisting our data

In order to tie all this together, we'll now look at how we can persist the data; we start by making a call to `Helper.saveRecipes()`, which currently doesn't exist. Head on over to `Helper.swift` and add the following functions there:

```
// Add Recipe
static func saveRecipes(recipes: [RecipeModel]) {
    let data = try! JSONEncoder().encode(recipes)
    UserDefaults.standard.set(data, forKey: "recipes")
}
// Gets List of Saved Recipes
static func getRecipes() -> [RecipeModel] {
    if let data = UserDefaults.standard.data(forKey: "recipes") {
        let array = try! JSONDecoder().decode([RecipeModel].self, from:
data)
        return array
    }
    return [RecipeModel]()
}
```

We've added two helper functions similar to those we created earlier for persisting our favorites. `saveRecipe()` accepts an array of `RecipeModel()` and `getRecipes()` returns an array of `RecipeModel()`.

Let's make another quick change to our mock data helper too in order to add in any recipes we've created manually through our app; this will allow our app to have some dummy and real data during development and testing. Make the following highlighted change inside `mockRecipes()`:

```
    recipies.append(contentsOf: getRecipes())
    return recipies
}
```

When creating an array of mock recipes, we simply append any recipes that we've created in our app to this array in order to include them in our list.

However, we'll need to make one minor change to the way we read in our recipes over in our `SceneDelegate.swift` file. Head on over there now and make the following highlighted change:

```
let appData = AppData()
appData.recipes = Helper.getRecipes()

let contentView = ContentView()
```

Here, we have removed the call to our `mockData()` and replaced it with our actual `getRecipes` function.

Making the save

This has been a lot to take in so far, but you're doing great. Just one more piece of the puzzle to solve now... yep, you guessed it! Let's add the `Save` button to tie it all together!

We'll start by adding another `Button()` to our form. Add the following highlighted code at the end of the `Form()` just after the picker view and underneath the `navigationBarTitle()`:

```
} // Closing Form Brace
.navigationBarTitle("Add Recipe")
.navigationBarItems(trailing:
    Button(action: {
        self.saveRecipe()
        self.presentationMode.wrappedValue.dismiss()
    }) {
        Text("Save")
    }
)
```

Here, we've created a new button that will sit just outside of our form and give it a Text View labeled `Save`. As part of the button's action, we've added a call to two functions:

```
self.saveRecipe()
self.presentationMode.wrappedValue.dismiss()
```

`saveRecipe()` is the save function we just created, allowing us to persist our recipe. Next is the dismissal of our sheet.

In order to understand this a little better, let's first add a new variable to our `AddRecipeView` struct:

```
@Environment(\.presentationMode) var presentationMode
```

This `@Environment` variable allows us to keep track of the current state of our presented view, and in turn, should we wish to dismiss it, we can simply call the following:

```
self.presentationMode.wrappedValue.dismiss()
```

Now when your SwiftUI sheet is dismissed, our `ContentView()` will automatically reload its state (based on the two-way binding to `showAddRecipe`) and the `appData.recipes` will load in the updated list of recipes from the `@EnvironmentObject` we created in the previous chapter.

Now it's time to have a play. Fire up the simulator and add a recipe, filling in all the required details. Press Save and restart the app. Your new recipe should be there for all to see! You can even click on the recipe and see the full details in the `RecipeDetailView()`.

In this section, we took everything we built in the previous sections and saved it into our app. We learned how to use `UserDefaults` in order to persist and retrieve images, and the importance of formatting our image correctly, because we can't always trust the size of the original source.

Summary

We've covered a lot in this chapter. We've built a brand-new view that makes use of a **Form** View and **sections** to allow us to easily create an input form for our recipes. We covered various types of images and how our old friend `UIImage` comes into play with SwiftUI, allowing us to take a photo from our library and not only insert it into our View but persist and retrieve it when we need to.

We also covered how SwiftUI can integrate into UIKit's existing framework using components that may not necessarily be available yet from SwiftUI, or simply custom components that were created previously and may still add some value.

In the next chapter, we'll be going through this in a little more detail and showing more of the behind the scenes of what we can achieve with SwiftUI in existing applications, including network connectivity.

Questions

1. In our `TextField`, why do we pass in a `@State` variable for our text?
2. What is the obvious difference between creating a View and a custom modifier?
3. What modifier do we use to add items to the navigation bar?
4. What is required for our default picker to push to a page of options?
5. Why do we care about the size of our Image Views?

8
Networking and Linking to Your Existing App Logic

Whether you're creating a brand new app or building on an existing one, with the best will in the world, at some point, you'll always need to tap into some form of existing framework or legacy code. Regardless of what people may say... that's actually okay.

In this chapter, we'll touch on the basics of networking in SwiftUI and how you might link into an existing networking approach that's commonly used by most iOS apps. Then, we'll deep dive into how we can use and harness existing UIKit Controls and gracefully yet powerfully implement these directly into our SwiftUI app.

The following topics will be covered in this chapter:

- Basic networking in SwiftUI
- Integrating UIViews with UIViewRepresentable
- Integrating ViewControllers with UIViewControllerRepresentable
- Other representable protocols

Technical requirements

For this chapter, you'll need to download Xcode version 11.3 or above from the Apple Mac App Store. You'll also need to be running the latest version of macOS (Catalina or above).

Simply search for Xcode in the App Store and select and download the latest version.

Launch Xcode and follow any additional installation instructions that your system may prompt you for. Once Xcode has fully launched, you'll be ready to go.

Basic networking in SwiftUI

In this section, we'll start by covering networking with SwiftUI. We touched on the basics of how we could implement this using the MVVN pattern back in Chapter 3, *Building Layout and Structure*, but now that we're building our app, let's look at making an actual networking call to retrieve some data that we can use in our recipe app.

Creating our network helper

Let's start by taking a look at what data we are going to get back from our call. We'll use a publicly open API called `https://source.unsplash.com/` that will generate a placeholder image for our recipe on the off chance we've not got a photo at hand.

This is a very simple API that is generated based on the structure of the URL. For example, if you wanted a placeholder image that's 300 x 200 in size and categorized as *food*, you would simply access the following
URL: `https://source.unsplash.com/300x200/?food`.

If you refresh the URL, you'll see a different image – nice!

Now, let's see how and where we are going to add this to our app. First, we'll create a new Helper class called `NetworkHelper` by highlighting the group name in the File Tree, right-clicking it, and selecting **New File**. Select **SwiftUI View** from the **User Interface** options and click **Next**. Call your new file `NetworkHelper.swift` and click **Create.**

Copy the following function into the class. We'll go through this line by line:

```
static func loadData(url: URL, completion: @escaping (UIImage?) -> ()) {
    URLSession.shared.dataTask(with: url) { data, response, error in
        guard let data = data, error == nil else {
            completion(nil)
            return
        }
        completion(UIImage(data: data))
    }.resume()
}
```

The preceding function is very basic, yet very powerful in what it does: it accepts a type of URL (which we'll create shortly from a URL string), makes the call asynchronously, and, if successful, returns a type of `UIImage`. This type of function is known as a closure and, when called, will allow any subsequent calls and logic to continue prior to receiving a response (or finishing its current operation, depending on what you are using it for).

Invoking our network request

With this set up, let's head on over to `AddRecipeDetailView.swift` and plug it in.

Create the following private function. This calls our new `NetworkHelper` closure, which will assign a `UIImage` to our `@State libraryImage` property:

```
private func getRandomImage() {
    guard let url = URL(string:
"https://source.unsplash.com/300x200/?food") else {
        return
    }
    NetworkHelper.loadData(url: url) { (image) in
        self.libraryImage = image
    }
}
```

Should our closure successfully return a `UIImage`, our `libraryImage` will update and SwiftUI will reload the current state. With our existing logic in place, we should see the randomly generated image courtesy of `source.unsplash.com` show up in our app!

But before we try this out, we'll need to hook up the preceding function to actually run anything. Let's make this simple and add another bar button item to our Navigation View. Make the following highlighted amendments in the current file:

```
.navigationBarTitle("Add Recipe")
.navigationBarItems(leading:
    Button(action: {
        self.getRandomImage()
    }) {
        Text("Random Image")
    }, trailing:
    Button(action: {
        self.saveRecipe()
        self.presentationMode.wrappedValue.dismiss()
    }) {
        Text("Save")
    }
)
```

Here, we've added a new leading button to our existing bar button item list, which in turn calls our new function, getRandomImage(). If you haven't already, resume the automatic previews canvas. You should see the following output:

Looks good, right? Now, fire up the simulator and try it for yourself. Click a random image (as many times as you like to get your desired image), enter a recipe, and click **Save**. You should successfully see your new recipe and be able to view its details, along with the new image you randomly generated:

In this section, we learned how to make basic networking calls in SwiftUI by hooking up a potentially exciting networking interface and adding an image directly into our SwiftUI code, with very little effort.

In the next section, we'll take a look at existing UIKit controls and how we can use them directly within our SwiftUI application. We'll look at one of the controls we used in Chapter 7, *Creating a Form with States and Data Binding*, and break this down to see how we can make use of UIViewRepresentable to achieve this.

Integrating UIViews with UIViewRepresentable

With most existing or legacy apps, you'll have specific UI features that you'll not only want to use but need to use to maintain parity with when introducing SwiftUI.

In this section, we'll take a look at `TextHelper()`, which we brought in from Chapter 7, *Creating a Form with States and Data Binding*, and how we made use of `UITextField`, which gave us the option to use `MultiLine TextFields` within our app. This section will cover the basics of the `UIViewRepresentable` protocol and the coordinator in order to successfully bind UIKit controls with SwiftUI.

Implementing UIViewRepresentable

We'll start by covering how we set up and use the `UIViewRepresentable` protocol. Head on over to `TextHelper.swift`, where we can use the `TextView` we imported for reference.

First of all, you'll need to create a struct that you intend to use to represent the UIKit View you want to house. This will need to extend the `UIViewRepresentable` protocol with the following functions. Add the following code just outside of the `TextView` struct in `TextHelper.swift`:

```
struct TestRepresentableView: UIViewRepresentable {
    @Binding var text: String

    func makeUIView(context: Context) -> UITextView {
        return UITextView()
    }
    func updateUIView(_ uiView: UITextView, context: Context) {
        uiView.text = text
    }
}
```

We'll go through them one at a time:

```
func makeUIView(context: Context) -> UITextView
```

The `makeUIView()` function will create and return our UIKit View ready for SwiftUI. The only thing you'll need to change here is the return type (in this case, `UITextView`) so that it matches the type of UIKit View you want to represent. For the moment, we are just returning an instance of `UITextView()`:

```
func updateUIView(_ uiView: UITextView, context: Context)
```

`updateView()` will run whenever your view us updated. Again, the type of View being passed in must be that of the View you're trying to represent.

In this function, we'll simply assign the value of *text*. We pass this from our `TextView` struct back to the `uiView` parameter that's being passed into the `updateUIView` function.

And that's basically it! Now, we can use our new `TestView()` function anywhere we like in our SwiftUI app, just as if it was another SwiftUI control:

```
@State var testString = ""
var body: some View {
    TestRepresentableView(text: $testString)
        .font(.body)
}
```

Next, we'll take a look at how we can further customize our `UIViewRepresentable` and coordinators to our specification's needs.

Customizing our UIViewRepresentable and coordinators

Now that we've got the basics up and running, we'll take a closer look at our `TextView` in `TextHelper.swift`. You'll see a very similar pattern to what we had previously but with some added extras – don't worry about these; we'll go through them very shortly. For now, let's start by taking a closer look at our `makeUIView()` function. Notice that we've got a lot more going on in there than our previous example:

```
func makeUIView(context: Context) -> UITextView {

    let textView = UITextView()
    textView.delegate = context.coordinator

    textView.font = UIFont.preferredFont(forTextStyle: .body)
    textView.isScrollEnabled = true
    textView.isEditable = true
    textView.isUserInteractionEnabled = true
```

```
        return textView
    }
```

All in all, it's nothing special – we're just setting up a couple of properties on our `UITextView` in the same way we would set our modifiers in SwiftUI. However, you'll need to pay attention to one particular line, which is highlighted in the preceding code.

A `UITextView` can accept a delegate of `UITextViewDelegate` – for those of you who are familiar with the existing delegate pattern, you'll know that we can still make good use of this from within our `UIViewRepresentable`.

 For more information on the Delegation pattern used by Apple, see the relevant link in the *Further reading* section.

To implement our `UITextViewDelegate`, we'll need to make the following changes. We'll continue this with the `TestRepresentableView` we started earlier.

Inside the `TestRepresentableView` struct, create a class called `Coordinator`. This will need to extend `NSObject`, as well as the delegate we want to use (in this case, `UITextViewDelegate`):

```
class Coordinator : NSObject, UITextViewDelegate
```

Once created, we'll need to add a property called `parent` that will be of the `TestRepresentableView` type. This is our link to the parent view from our coordinator:

```
var parent: TextView
```

Next, we'll add the highlighted initializer for our coordinator:

```
var parent: TextView

init(_ uiTextView: TextView) {
    self.parent = uiTextView
}
```

Finally, we'll add our required delegate methods for our `UITextView`:

```
func textView(_ textView: UITextView, shouldChangeTextIn range: NSRange,
replacementText text: String) -> Bool {
    return true
}

func textViewDidChange(_ textView: UITextView) {
    self.parent.text = textView.text
}
```

These are a couple of commonly used delegate methods for a `UITextField`.

Basically, `shouldChangeTextIn` is called whenever a user types in a new character or deletes one and returns a Boolean based on its operation. `textViewDidChange` is called when text is changed, thus allowing us to update the `parent` property.

Next, we'll need to initialize the `Coordinator` in our `TestRepresentableView`. To do this, we simply add the following function inside our struct (not in the coordinator class):

```
func makeCoordinator() -> Coordinator {
    Coordinator(self)
}
```

We're almost done! Take a look and our new representable view and compare this to the TextView we implemented in the previous chapter. Notice we're missing one last piece to the puzzle... that's right – we can now hook up our coordinator to the delegate property in the `makeUIView()` function!

Go ahead and make the following highlighted changes:

```
func makeUIView(context: Context) -> UITextView {
    let textView = UITextView()
    textView.delegate = context.coordinator
    return textView
}
```

All we've done here is create an instance of `UITextView` as a variable and assigned `context.coordinator` to its delegate. Go ahead: try and add your new `TestRepresentableView` into your project – it should work a treat!

In this section, we covered and compared how we previously used a `UITextFiled` in our app by making use of the `UIViewRepresentable` protocol. We learned how `UIViewRepresentable` is simply a wrapper that allows us to harness any UIKit Control and implement this into our SwiftUI project. We also saw how UIKit Controls that make use of the delegate pattern can also be used by making use of a coordinator.

In the next section, we'll create a brand new UIKit control using `UIViewRepresentable` that we can use in our recipe app.

Integrating ViewControllers with UIViewControllerRepresentable

In this section, we'll take a look at the `ImageHelper()` we brought in from `Chapter 7,` *Creating a Form with States and Data Binding* and how we made use of `UIImagePickerController`, which gave us the option to choose a photo from our library to use within our app. This section will cover the basics of `UIViewControllerRepresentable` and the coordinator, in order to successfully bind a `UIViewController` to our app.

Implementing UIViewControllerRepresentable

Let's start by heading on over and taking a look at our implementation of `ImageHelper.swift`. Much like `UIViewRepresentable`, the layout and required functions are pretty much the same. So, for this reason, we won't go through and create another `UIViewControllerRepresentable` struct; instead, we'll just cover how we created `ImagePickerViewController` function by function.

First of all, let's take a look at our `makeUIViewController()` function. Much like the `makeUIView()` function, here, we create an instance of `UIViewController` we want to use and return this to SwiftUI so that it can use it:

```
func makeUIViewController(context:
UIViewControllerRepresentableContext<ImagePickerViewController>) ->
UIImagePickerController {

    let imagePicker = UIImagePickerController()
    imagePicker.sourceType =
UIImagePickerController.SourceType.photoLibrary
    imagePicker.allowsEditing = false
```

```
        imagePicker.delegate = context.coordinator
        return imagePicker

    }
```

Again, this is pretty standard stuff – we've created an instance of
`UIImagePickerController()` where we can set the `sourceType` of our picker (our
photo library), our delegate (again, this is hooked up to our coordinator), and the
`allowsEditing` property – which is just personal preference as to how we want our
`ImagePickerController` to work.

Now, let's take a look at `updateUIViewContoller()`. Once again, the same principles
apply to this as they did to `updateUIView()` in the previous section, but with a slight
difference to what we implement inside. Let's take a look:

```
        func updateUIViewController(_ uiViewController:
    UIImagePickerController,
                        context:
    UIViewControllerRepresentableContext<ImagePickerViewController>) {
        }
```

That's right! It's empty. Due to the nature of how `UIImagePickerController()` works,
there is no need to update the UI at any specific time. This function will still get called and
if you wanted, you could add something in here (such as analytics). However, for the
purpose of this book, it's good as it is.

Continuing with `ImageHelper.swift`, once again, we see our `makeCoordinator()`
function serving the same purpose as it did in the `UIViewRepresentable` example:

```
    func makeCoordinator() -> Coordinator {
        Coordinator(self)
    }
```

The exact same principles apply with our actual coordinator class too, acting as a wrapper
for our `UIImagePickerControllerDelegate()` delegate:

```
    class Coordinator: NSObject, UIImagePickerControllerDelegate,
    UINavigationControllerDelegate {
        var parent: ImagePickerViewController
        init(_ parent: ImagePickerViewController) {
            self.parent = parent
        }
        func imagePickerController(_ picker: UIImagePickerController,
    didFinishPickingMediaWithInfo info: [UIImagePickerController.InfoKey :
    Any]) {
            . . .
```

```
        }
        func imagePickerControllerDidCancel(_ picker: UIImagePickerController)
    {
            ...
        }
    }
```

Before we continue, let's go back to the top of `ImageHelper.swift` and have a look at the variables we've created:

```
@Binding var presentationMode: PresentationMode
@Binding var image: UIImage?
```

One of these variables is our `UIImage`. We'll pass this into `UIViewControllerRepresentable` so we can assign it to the image picked by the user (this happens in the `didFinishPickingMediaWithInfo` delegate within our coordinator). Notice that this is using two-way binding so that, once our image has been assigned, SwiftUI can update its View.

Next is our `presentationMode` variable. This is required to allow us to dismiss `UIViewControllerRepresentable` once the picker has finished doing its job. As you may recall from Chapter 7, *Creating a Form with States and Data Binding*, we used this in order to dismiss our `AddRecipeView` sheet.

Now, if we compare this with the `UIViewRepresentable` we created, with the exception of what control or `ViewController` we are implementing, the structure is pretty much like for like, apart from one last struct we created at the bottom of `ImageHelper.swift`:

```
struct ImagePicker : View {
    @Binding var image: UIImage?
    @Environment(\.presentationMode) var presentationMode
    var body: some View {
        ImagePickerViewController(presentationMode: presentationMode,
    image: $image)
    }
}
```

Since we need to know the current *presentation mode* of our SwiftUI View in order to successfully dismiss our `ImagePickerViewController`, we'll need to get a reference to the `@Environment` mode for the current presentation of the View.

Unfortunately, we can't have this within our `UIViewControllerRepresentable` struct. Only a binding to a value being passed in (seen in the preceding code) is allowed.

For this, we create a small SwiftUI View that calls our `ImagePickerViewController`, passing in the current `@Environment` presentation. Now, within `ImagePickerViewController`, we can successfully dismiss the View as/when we need to.

Let's tie all this together by taking another look at how we implemented this in our `AddRecipeView` View:

```
.sheet(isPresented: $showingImagePicker) {
    ImagePicker(image: self.$libraryImage)
}.buttonStyle(PlainButtonStyle())
```

As highlighted in the preceding code, we can see how our `ImagePicker` is easily integrated into our app.

In this section, we learned about the differences between `UIViewRepresentable` and `UIViewControllerRepresentable` and how both follow a very similar architectural pattern. We saw how we can handle a `UIViewController` being dismissed within a `UIViewControllerRepresentable` and how we can create a stub View to achieve this.

Other representable protocols

So far in this chapter, we've covered the two main representable protocols, `UIViewRepresentable` and `UIViewControllerRepresentable`, but we can also conform to other variations of the representable protocol to allow for even more versatility within SwiftUI.

In this section, we'll briefly touch on other options available to us and how they can also be used in a similar way to `UIViewRepresentable` and `UIViewControllerRepresentable`.

Options for macOS

With catalyst being announced alongside SwiftUI and the option for developers to build native macOS apps straight off the back of their iPadOS apps, it only makes sense to allow the same behavior to be able to create SwiftUI apps in macOS just like you can on iOS and iPadOS.

With almost identical options to iOS, macOS offers the following in terms of the representable protocol:

```
struct TestRepresentableView: NSViewRepresentable {
    func makeNSView(context:
NSViewRepresentableContext<TestRepresentableView>) -> NSTextView {
        return NSTextView()
    }
    func updateNSView(_ nsView: NSTextView, context:
NSViewRepresentableContext<TestRepresentableView>) {
        // ...
    }
    static func dismantleNSView(_ nsView: NSTextView, coordinator: ()) {
        // ...
    }
}
```

The preceding code is an example of macOS's View Representable, again making use of the make, update, and dismantle functions.

The following is an example of how macOS's ViewController Representable is implemented:

```
struct TestRepresentableViewController: NSViewControllerRepresentable {
    func makeNSViewController(context:
NSViewControllerRepresentableContext<TestRepresentableViewController>) ->
NSViewController {
        return NSViewController()
    }
    func updateNSViewController(_ nsViewController: NSViewController,
context:
NSViewControllerRepresentableContext<TestRepresentableViewController>) {
        // ...
    }
    static func dismantleNSViewController(_ nsViewController:
NSViewController, coordinator: ()) {
        // ...
    }
}
```

Again, the preceding code is an example of macOS's ViewController Representable, making use of the make, update, and dismantle functions.

Options for watchOS

Apple's watchOS can also get in on the action, with an almost identical pattern being used to implement the representable protocol throughout the watch development process. It's important to bear this in mind as we'll be covering this later in Chapter 11, *SwiftUI on WatchOS*, where this will play a slightly bigger part:

```
struct TestRepresentableViewController: WKInterfaceObjectRepresentable {
    func makeWKInterfaceObject(context:
WKInterfaceObjectRepresentableContext<TestRepresentableViewController>) ->
WKInterfaceTextField {
        // ...
    }
    func updateWKInterfaceObject(_ wkInterfaceObject: WKInterfaceTextField,
context:
WKInterfaceObjectRepresentableContext<TestRepresentableViewController>) {
        // ...
    }
    static func dismantleWKInterfaceObject(_ wkInterfaceObject:
WKInterfaceTextField, coordinator: ()) {
        // ...
    }
}
```

As familiar as this pattern seems, the consistency within each device is key to the success of multi-platform apps for iOS, iPadOS, watchOS, and macOS.

In this section, we covered alternative options regarding how we can use the representable protocol in SwiftUI across the various Apple platforms and learned how the patterns we created in the previous sections can be used in the same way.

In the next chapter, we'll take what we have learned here about representable protocols and adopt them in order to use Apple Maps within our recipe app to pinpoint the origin of our recipes.

Summary

In this chapter, we covered how linking SwiftUI to existing logic and UIKit frameworks can be achieved. First, we looked at how we integrate into a very common approach for networking by using `NetworkHelper` along with `URLSession` to perform our network request. From this, we were successfully able to update our SwiftUI View with ease.

Next, we took a deep dive into two of the main representable protocols, `UIViewRepresentable` and `UIViewControllerRepresentable`, and stepped through how we previously used these in Chapter 7, *Creating a Form with States and Data Binding*, in order to implement existing UIKit controls. We covered the differences between using both and understood why we need to take a slightly different approach for `UIViewControllerRepresentable` in order to dismiss the ViewController, should we need to.

Finally, we briefly covered the remaining available representable protocols that are available for watchOS and macOS.

In the next section, we'll take a look at adding Apple Maps to our SwiftUI project by utilizing `UIViewRepresentable` and `UIViewControllerRepresentable`.

Questions

1. Why is it important that we use two-way binding when loading remote images?
2. Why should we use `UIViewRepresentable`?
3. Why should we use `UIViewControllerRepresentable`?
4. When would we use the coordinator pattern?
5. What did we do differently when creating `UIViewControllerRepresentable` and why?

Further reading

- **Delegate Design Patterns:** https://developer.apple.com/documentation/swift/cocoa_design_patterns/using_delegates_to_customize_object_behavior
- **UITextView:** https://developer.apple.com/documentation/uikit/uitextviewdelegate/1618630-textview
- **UITextView Delegate:** https://developer.apple.com/documentation/uikit/uitextviewdelegate/1618599-textviewdidchange
- **UIPickerView Delegate:** https://developer.apple.com/documentation/uikit/uipickerviewdelegate
- **UIViewRepresentable:** https://developer.apple.com/documentation/swiftui/uiviewrepresentable
- **UIViewControllerRepresentable:** https://developer.apple.com/documentation/swiftui/uiviewcontrollerrepresentable

Maps and Location Services

9

In this chapter, we'll be covering Maps and Location Services within iOS and how we can integrate this into our SwiftUI app. We'll learn how to use Apple's built-in MapKit framework to display maps directly in our app and add annotations (or pins as they are sometimes known as) to specific locations throughout.

We'll also cover Core Location and see how Xcode's cool feature of location spoofing allows us to simulate various locations from around the world and update our SwiftUI app dynamically.

Finally, we'll tie all this together and use what we've learned to display recipe locations on our map with the ability to select them and filter our recipes.

The following topics will be covered in this chapter:

- Adding a Map with MapKit control
- Creating our first pin
- Identifying our location
- Piecing it all together

Technical requirements

For this chapter, you'll need to download Xcode version 11.3 or above from the Apple Mac App Store. You'll also need to be running the latest version of macOS (Catalina or above).

Simply search for Xcode in the App Store and select and download the latest version.

Launch Xcode and follow any additional installation instructions that your system may prompt you for. Once Xcode has fully launched, you're ready to go.

Adding a Map with MapKit control

As we learned in the previous chapter, Chapter 8, *Networking and Linking to Your Existing App Logic*, working with existing app logic will require you from time to time to make use of 0f `UIViewRepresentable` and/or `UIViewControllerRepresentable` when implementing existing UIKit features. MapKit is currently no exception to this, and in this section, we'll start to build our `MapView` using this methodology. We'll create a `UIViewRepresentable` struct around the current MapKit control and add this directly into our SwiftUI recipe app.

Implementing MapKit

We'll start by creating a new SwiftUI View; we'll create a new file in our Xcode project called `RecipeMapView` by highlighting the group name in the file tree, then right-clicking and selecting **New File**. Select **SwiftUI View** from the **User Interface** options and click **Next**. Call your new file `RecipeMapView.swift` and click **Create**.

Now we'll create another helper file called `MapKitHelper` by highlighting the group name in the file tree, then right-clicking and selecting **New File**. Select **Cocoa Touch Class** from the **User Interface** options and click **Next**. Call your new file `MapKitHelper.swift` and click **Create**.

Inside our helper, make the following changes. Note the `import` statement at the top of the file; this is needed to tell our project that we intend to use MapKit inside our class or struct:

```
import UIKit
import SwiftUI
import MapKit

struct MapView: UIViewRepresentable {

  @State var lat = 0.0
  @State var long = 0.0

  func makeUIView(context: Context) -> MKMapView {
    MKMapView(frame: .zero)
  }
  func updateUIView(_ view: MKMapView, context: Context){
    let coordinate = CLLocationCoordinate2D(
      latitude: lat, longitude: long)
    let span = MKCoordinateSpan(latitudeDelta: 2.0, longitudeDelta: 2.0)
    let region = MKCoordinateRegion(center: coordinate, span: span)
    view.setRegion(region, animated: true)
```

```
    }
  }
```

Let's go through this again; much like the `UIViewRepresentable` helpers we created in `Chapter 8`, *Networking and Linking to Your Existing App Logic,* we conform our struct to the `UIViewRepresentable` protocol, and we have `makeUIView` and `updateUIView` functions that house our logic to generate a MapKit `UIView`.

For this book, we don't need to go into too much detail on how we actually implement a MapKit `UIView`; we'll only touch on the areas relevant to what we need.

First, of all, take a quick look at the `updateUIView` function; note that we create an instance of `CLLocationCoordinate2D`. Basically, this is where we drop in our coordinates (latitude and longitude) to determine what is shown on our map.

As you can see, inside our struct we've created two variables for each of these values, both of which I have highlighted in the following snippet:

```
var lat = 0.0
var lon = 0.0

// ...
func updateUIView(_ view: MKMapView, context: Context){
  let coordinate = CLLocationCoordinate2D(
    latitude: lat, longitude: lon)
  let span = MKCoordinateSpan(latitudeDelta: 2.0, longitudeDelta: 2.0)
  let region = MKCoordinateRegion(center: coordinate, span: span)
  view.setRegion(region, animated: true)
}
```

For now, that's just enough to get us going. Let's now add this to our `RecipeMapView` to see this in action.

Adding a MapKit View to SwiftUI

Head on back over to `RecipeMapView.swift` and you should see the automatically generated template complete with a body and a text view.

Make the following change to add the `MapView` we just created:

```
struct RecipeMapView: View {
  var body: some View {
    MapView(lat: 37.3327177, lon: -122.0753671)
  }
}
```

I've highlighted in the preceding code the main change we've made – we simply added in our `MapView` struct and passed in the latitude and longitude as parameters.

 Latitude and longitude is a coordinate system by means of which the position or location of any place on the Earth's surface can be determined.

If you haven't already done so, press **Resume** on the automatic preview window to see the map being added to our canvas.

Now normally, we'd need to hook up our new `RecipeMapView` in order to see the map in action, but I'm going to introduce you to a new feature in Xcode 11 and SwiftUI that will allow us to initialize our `MapView` as if it were running on the simulator.

In the bottom-right corner of the canvas, you'll see the following icon that looks like a *play* button – this is called *Live* mode:

Go ahead and hit this button, and within a moment or so you should see MapKit initialize within our `RecipeMapView` and display on our screen. You're also able to control the map by dragging (clicking and holding your primary mouse or trackpad button) and moving it around–go on, have a play:

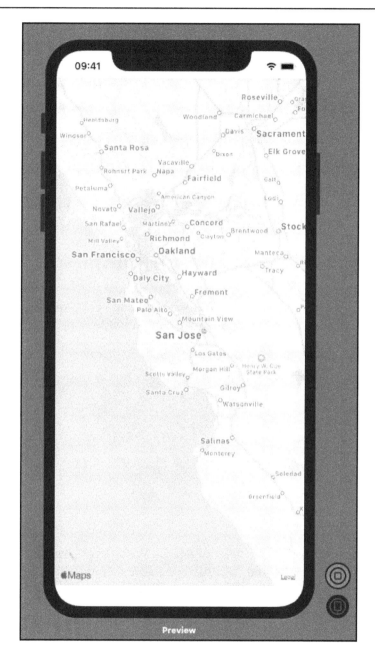

And that's how easy it is! Again, by using the techniques we learned in `Chapter 8`, *Networking and Linking to Your Existing App Logic*, we've been able to easily create and implement a `MapKitUI` in SwiftUI with very little effort at all.

In the next section, we'll create our very first pin to add to our map so we can pinpoint the location of one of our recipes.

Creating our first pin

Now that we've successfully implemented MapKit directly into our SwiftUI View, let's get a bit creative by adding some pins (or annotations, as they are officially known) to our `RecipeMapView`. We'll start by adding basic annotations to our map using some mock data that we'll generate for our automatic preview canvas and then we'll look at how we can customize each annotation to show details of the recipes we have for that specific area.

Adding your first annotation (pin)

We'll start by heading on over to `MapHelper.swift`, where we'll create a new class called `AnnotationPin`. This class will be a custom subclass of `MKAnnotation`. We're creating a subclass as we'd like to customize the annotation later on.

Add the following at the footer of our `MapHelper.swift` for now:

```
class AnnotationPin: NSObject, MKAnnotation {
  let title: String?
  let subtitle: String?
  let coordinate: CLLocationCoordinate2D
  init(title: String?, subtitle: String?, coordinate:
CLLocationCoordinate2D) {
    self.title = title
    self.subtitle = subtitle
    self.coordinate = coordinate
  }
}
```

The preceding is a basic subclass of `MKAnnotation`. We've even overwritten the base properties of `title`, `subtitle`, and `coordinate` so we can initialize these ourselves along with anything additional we want later.

Still within our `MapHelper.swift` file, but back up to our `UIViewRepresentable` implementation, we'll make the following highlighted change within the `updateUIView` function:

```
func updateUIView(_ view: MKMapView, context: Context){
  let coordinate = CLLocationCoordinate2D(latitude: lat, longitude: long)
  let span = MKCoordinateSpan(latitudeDelta: 2.0, longitudeDelta: 2.0)
```

```
    let region = MKCoordinateRegion(center: coordinate, span: span)
    view.setRegion(region, animated: true)
    view.addAnnotations(locations)


  }
```

addAnnotaions takes an array of `MKAnnotation` (or an array of objects that is a subclass of it). We'll now need to create a variable for this array in our struct. Add on the following just after the `lat` and `long` declarations:

```
    var annotations: [AnnotationPin]
```

If you now head back over to `RecipeMapView.swift`, you'll see that our `MapView` now requires an additional parameter; let's fix this by creating some mock data for our annotations.

Head on over to `Helper.swift` and create the following helper method (you may want to copy and paste this from the sample project):

```
    static func getMockLocations()-> [AnnotationPin] {
      var annotations = [AnnotationPin]()
      annotations.append(AnnotationPin(name: "Recipe One",
                    locationName: "San Jose",
                      coordinate: CLLocationCoordinate2D(latitude:
37.3327177, longitude:
                                            -122.0753671)))
      annotations.append(AnnotationPin(name: "Recipe Two",
                    locationName: "San Francisco",
                      coordinate: CLLocationCoordinate2D(latitude: 37.6160179,
      longitude:
                                    -122.3946882)))
      return annotations
    }
```

Here we are just creating an array of our `AnnotationPin` with a dummy title and subtitle and some random coordinates, as this will be enough to demonstrate and test our `MapView` with annotations.

Now head back over to `RecipeMapView.swift` and satisfy the missing parameter by referencing the new `Helper` function we created:

```
    struct RecipeMapView: View {
      var body: some View {
        MapView(lat: 37.3327177, lon: -122.0753671, annotations:
    Helper.getMockLocations())
      }
    }
```

Resume the automatic preview canvas (remembering to go into 'live' mode) and you should see your pins drop on, just like in the following screenshot:

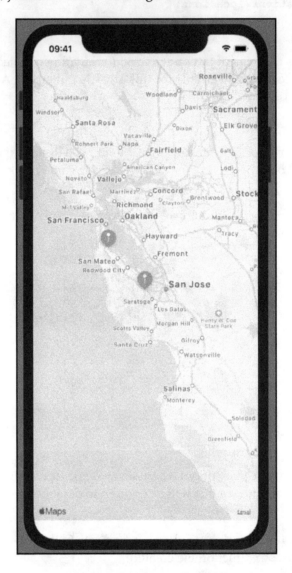

And that's how easy it is to add annotations to your MapKit `UIView` built through SwiftUI. Next, we'll look at customizing the annotations with details about our recipes in that location.

Creating custom annotations

For this next part, we're going to create a custom annotation where we can display some details about our recipe. You'll notice that we passed a title and subtitle to our `AnnotationPin` class–this can now be displayed as a custom annotation, along with a custom image of our choosing.

In order to achieve this, we'll need to make use of a MapKit delegate function called `viewFor` annotation. Let's start by hooking up the `MKMapViewDelegate` to our `UIViewRepresentable` class, as shown in the following:

```
class MapViewCoordinator: NSObject, MKMapViewDelegate {
  var parent: MapView
  init(_ control: MapView) {
    self.parent = control
  }
  func mapView(_ mapView: MKMapView, viewFor annotation: MKAnnotation) ->
MKAnnotationView? {
    let annotationView = MKAnnotationView(annotation: annotation,
reuseIdentifier: "customView")
    annotationView.canShowCallout = true
    annotationView.image = UIImage(systemName: "book.fill")
    return annotationView
  }
}
```

I've highlighted some areas of interest in the preceding code block, but again we create a reference to the `parent MapView` and initializer and then the required delegate function from `MKMapViewDelegate`.

The code inside of `viewFor annotation` is standard code for implementing a custom annotation view. The only bit we want to concentrate on is the image we're assigning. Again we make use of the widely available SF Symbols in order to choose a font for our pin.

Now head on back up to our `UIViewRepresentable` implementation–can you remember what we need to add next? That's right, we need to add in our `makeCoordinator()` function:

```
func makeCoordinator() -> MapViewCoordinator{
  MapViewCoordinator(self)
}
```

Next, we assign this to the delegate property in `updateUIView()`:

```
func updateUIView(_ view: MKMapView, context: Context){
  let coordinate = CLLocationCoordinate2D(latitude: lat, longitude: long)
```

```
    let span = MKCoordinateSpan(latitudeDelta: 2.0, longitudeDelta: 2.0)
    let region = MKCoordinateRegion(center: coordinate, span: span)
    view.setRegion(region, animated: true)
    view.addAnnotations(locations)
    view.delegate = context.coordinator
}
```

Now head on back over to `RecipeMapView.swift` and press **Resume** on the automatic preview canvas (making sure you're in 'Live' mode too). All going well, you should be able to see the following:

Clicking on each one should produce a popup, which in turn will give the details passed in from the mock data we created earlier. It looks great, right?

In this section, we learned how to create a model that can be passed into our `MapView` with details of a specific location and show that on our app using an annotation. We then went a step further and customized the annotation, again making use of the coordinator pattern we learned about in `Chapter 8`, *Networking and Linking to Your Exiting App Logic*.

In the next section, we'll take a look at how we can add logic to our `MapView` in order to determine our location and how we can simulate multiple locations using the simulator.

Identifying our location

In this section, we'll dive into `CoreLocation` and see how we can update our SwiftUI `RecipeMapView` to reflect a certain location when set. We'll again touch on the basics of the Combine framework in order to help us achieve this. As we are primarily working with the iOS simulator, we'll also explore the tools available to us in Xcode that allow us to simulate a specific location and see that reflected in our SwiftUI app immediately.

Creating our MapLocationManager

Our first job is to create a `MapLocationManager` class. This will house all the logic required to obtain our current (or simulated) location and pass the relevant details back up to our main view in order for them to be displayed in SwiftUI.

Let's start by creating a new class; we'll create a new file in our Xcode project called `RecipeMapView` by highlighting the group name in the file tree, then right-clicking and selecting **New File**. Select **Cocoa Touch Class** from the **User Interface** options and click **Next**. Call your new file `MapLocationManager.swift` (making sure this is a subclass of `NSObject`) and click **Create**.

First things first, let's import the required frameworks. Add the following to the top of your class:

```
import Foundation
import Combine
import CoreLocation
```

Now overwrite the automatically generated class with the following:

```
class MapLocationManager: NSObject, ObservableObject {
  private let locationManager = CLLocationManager()
  let objectWillChange = PassthroughSubject<Void, Never>()
  @Published var status: CLAuthorizationStatus? {
    willSet { objectWillChange.send() }
  }
  @Published var location: CLLocation? {
    willSet { objectWillChange.send() }
  }
  override init() {
    super.init()
    self.locationManager.delegate = self
    self.locationManager.requestWhenInUseAuthorization()
    self.locationManager.startUpdatingLocation()
  }
}
```

I've highlighted a couple of areas of interest in the preceding code block. First of all, note how we conform to the `ObservableObject` protocol. This is part of the Combine framework, as we'll want to monitor any changes made to this object (location changes, for example) and push these out to our SwiftUI View as and when needed.

We've next got two `@Published` variables declared (I'm not going to go too deep into the inner workings of the Combine framework – we'll just cover what it does as opposed to why it does it). Basically, this listens to when the particular variable has changed value and will announce (or **publish**) the change. Note in `willSet`, that we now call `.send()` on the `objectWillChange` property–this will tell any objects listening (objects prefixed with `@ObservableObject`) that there has been a change made.

Next, we have the standard `init()` function – there's nothing special in here, just standard code for setting up Core Location's `LocationManager` service. One thing to note is that we do set a delegate on `locationManager`–so let's add that in next:

```
extension MapLocationManager: CLLocationManagerDelegate {
  func locationManager(_ manager: CLLocationManager, didChangeAuthorization
status: CLAuthorizationStatus) {
    self.status = status
  }

  func locationManager(_ manager: CLLocationManager, didUpdateLocations
locations: [CLLocation]) {
    guard let location = locations.last else { return }
    self.location = location
  }
}
```

Extensions are a great place to keep delegate methods, as not only do they help separate out the logic in potentially large classes, but they can also be extracted to another file if needed. Here we have created an extension on our `LocationManager` and conformed this to the `CLLocationManagerDelegate` protocol.

Inside our extension, we have two `CLLocationManagerDelegate` functions, `didChangeAuthorization` and `didUpdateLocations`. For the purpose of this book, it's not vital that you fully understand the inner workings of these delegates, only that `didChangeAuthorization` is called when there is a change in authorization (asking for permission to get your location) and `didUpdateLocations` is called when your location has physically changed.

Hooking up our MapLocationManager to SwiftUI

Now let's head on back over to `RecipeMapView.swift` to make just a couple of small changes to our SwiftUI View in order to work with our `MapLocationManager`.

Let's start by adding a reference to our `MapLocationManager`. Looking back at the previous section, can you think of anything special/different that we'll need to do in order for this object to *listen* for changes...?

```
@ObservedObject var locationManager = MapLocationManager()
```

That's right, we'll need to prefix it with `@ObservedObject` in order for our Combine logic to kick in and make us aware of any changes to our location.

Once we've got that back in place, let's grab the latitude and longitude from `MapLocationManager` and pass them to our previously created `MapView`:

```
var body: some View {
    MapView(lat: locationManager.location?.coordinate.latitude ?? 0.0,
        lon: locationManager.location?.coordinate.longitude ?? 0.0,
        annotations: Helper.getMockLocations())
}
```

As you can see, it's a little long-winded and untidy to grab the latitude and longitude from our `MapLocationManager`, so we can fix this by creating a couple of computed properties either in our `MapLocationManager` class or inside our `MapRecipeView.swift` file. For now, let's create these where we are:

```
var latitude: Double {
    return locationManager.location?.coordinate.latitude ?? 0.0
}
var longitude: Double {
    return locationManager.location?.coordinate.longitude ?? 0.0
}
var body: some View {
    MapView(lat: latitude,
        lon: longitude,
        annotations: Helper.getMockLocations())
}
```

Much neater–all we need to do next is fire up the simulator and see this in action, but first, let's cover a couple of little minor tweaks we need to implement to make this happen.

Location permissions

When trying to get a user's location in iOS, we are required to ask the user's permission first–in order to do this, we need to tell the user why we are requesting the permissions. iOS will handle the asking of the questions, but we need to provide the question. We achieve this by adding an entry into our `info.plist` file.

To access the `info.plist`, head over to the file tree and select your project at the very top of the tree hierarchy, then in the main window select the **Info** tab–you should now see a list of keys already pre-populated by Xcode for our app:

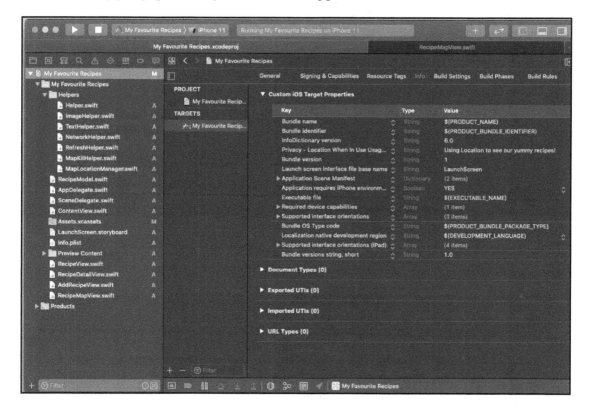

To add an entry, select the bottom key and press the + button next to the key name, then paste in the following key name:

```
NSLocationWhenInUseUsageDescription
```

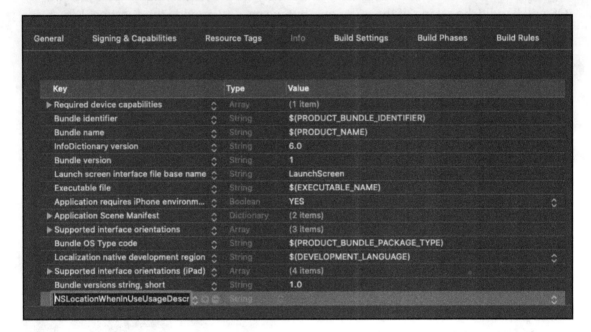

Once you've done that, enter the following as a value, keeping the `Type` set to `String`:

```
Using Location to see our yummy recipes!
```

Note that the value can be anything you want it to be at this stage, but for apps that are intended for the Apple App Store, the validation process from Apple is a little more strict. Try to give a more useful description when choosing this.

Once we've done that, we're ready to launch this in the simulator. Now, as we've not yet hooked our `RecipeMapView` into our app, we'll need to modify a line of code in our `SceneDelegate.swift` file as follows.

Find the following line:

```
let contentView = ContentView()
```

Now, change that line as follows:

```
let contentView = RecipeMapView()
```

Now launch the simulator, and, all going well, you should be presented with the following screen:

Updated permissions in iOS allow the user to decide if an app requiring Core Location services should only use their location whilst using the app (this permission will be granted for all subsequent uses of the app) or for only this one instance. For the purpose of this exercise, you are safe to choose the top option, **Allow While Using App**.

Once you've passed this screen, you are more than likely to be thrown somewhere in the ocean! But that's fine, as we are running in the simulator and Xcode isn't aware of our exact location.

Luckily, we can change that by simulating some predefined locations set in Xcode 11, whilst running in the simulator. Locate the following compass needle icon in the debugging toolbar (running along the bottom of the Xcode window):

If you click on it, you'll be given a drop-down list of multiple predefined locations that Xcode can simulate, which when selected will update your app instantly:

Go ahead, choose **San Francisco**. All going well, you should be animated off to California straight away... Did you notice anything else when you got there?

That's right, your annotations are there ready and waiting for us. How cool is that? Now try some more locations and see how well `CoreLocation` now works with our SwiftUI app (don't forget to revert the change in `SceneDelegate.swift` when you're done playing though).

In this section, we learned all about `CoreLocation` services and how we can create a simple yet effective class to handle all of our location-based data. We dove into some more of the Combine framework and saw how this helped us hook up our `MapLocationManger` to our SwiftUI frontend.

In the next section, we'll piece everything together and fully integrate our MapView into our recipe app!

Piecing it all together

Now that we've created our `MapView`, learned how to add pins (annotations), and learned how to customize our annotations too, we can integrate this straight into our recipe app.

In this section, we'll hook up our actual recipes to our `MapView`, placing an annotation on each country with a recipe. Then we'll use a custom annotation to list the country name and the number of recipes we have for that country.

We'll then take a look at the *call out accessory view* and how we can add a button that we'll be able to use to filter our `ContentView` list based on the country selected.

Finally, we'll add another navigation bar button item in order to clear our filter.

Updating our Helper classes

The first thing we need to do is create a couple of additional functions in our `Helper()` class in order to perform a latitude and longitude lookup for our `RecipeModel().origin` property.

Now, there's quite a bit here to type out, so you might just want to grab this from the sample project and copy it into yours.

We'll start by adding in a private function called `getCoordinates`. This function accepts a `String` parameter, which will be the country name:

```
private static func getCoordinates(country: String) ->
CLLocationCoordinate2D {

  switch country {
  case "Italy":
    return CLLocationCoordinate2D(latitude: 43.112221, longitude:
12.388889)
  case "Greece":
```

```
      return CLLocationCoordinate2D(latitude: 37.983810, longitude:
23.727539)
    case "UK":
      return CLLocationCoordinate2D(latitude: 53.483959, longitude:
-2.244644)
    default:
      return CLLocationCoordinate2D(latitude: 37.6160179, longitude:
-122.3946882)
    }

  }
```

In this function, we have a basic `switch` statement with a matched value to return against the parameter we passed in. I've removed some of the cases due to their size, so be sure to grab the file from the sample project for the full list.

As you can see, once matched, we basically return a new instance of `CLLocationCoordinate2D` with the latitude and longitude of that country (which I just searched for online).

Next, we'll create a public function called `getRecipeLocations`, which in turn will return an array of our `AnnotationPin()` class, which we created earlier:

```
static func getRecipeLocations(recipes: [RecipeModel]) -> [AnnotationPin] {

  var locations = [AnnotationPin]()
  let countries = Set(recipes.map{$0.origin})
  for country in countries {
    let count = recipes.filter {$0.origin == country }.count
    let subtitle = count > 1 ? "\(count) Recipes" : "\(count) Recipe"
    locations.append(AnnotationPin(title: country, subtitle: subtitle,
coordinate: Helper.getCoordinates(country: country)))
  }
  return locations

}
```

Now we could loop through each of our recipes and add these as annotations to our map, but that's not what we really want. We just want to place one annotation down if that country has a recipe, and advise on the number of recipes that the country has – nice and simple.

And that's what the preceding `Helper` function does: it grabs a list of all countries that have a recipe and adds each of them to an `AnnotationPin()`. It then performs a count on each country to see how many recipes a particular country has.

Once we have that information, we assign the country name to the `title` property and the count to the `subtitle` property.

Right, that's it for now with our `Helper` functions; next, we'll hook up our `MapView` to the rest of the app and make use of the `getRecipeLocations Helper` function we just created.

Hooking up our MapView

Okay, so we are going to add our `MapView` to the `ContentView()` of our app; we'll take the same approach as we did with the `AddRecipeView()` by adding this to our navigation bar button item. Head on over to `ContentView.swift` now and make the following highlighted change:

```
.navigationBarItems(leading: HStack {
  Button(action: {
    self.showMap.toggle()
  }) {
  Image(systemName: "map")
    .renderingMode(.original)
  }.sheet(isPresented: $showMap) {
    RecipeMapView()
  }}, trailing:
  Button(action: {
    self.showAddRecipe.toggle()
  }) {
    Image(systemName: "plus")
    .renderingMode(.original)
  }.sheet(isPresented: $showAddRecipe) {
    AddRecipeView().environmentObject(self.appData)
  })
```

As you can see from the preceding code block, the noticeable difference is that we've now separated out a leading and trailing bar button item (note that also I've added our leading button into an `HStack` – **spoiler alert**: we'll be adding another button here shortly).

Now head on over to `RecipeMapView()` and let's add in our new `Helper` function and other highlighted changes as follows:

```
var body: some View {
  NavigationView {
    MapView(lat: latitude,
        lon: longitude,
        annotations: Helper.getRecipeLocations())
```

```
            .navigationBarTitle(Text("Recipes of the World!"))
    }
}
```

We've wrapped our `MapView` inside a `NavigationView`. Now we can add in a navigation title bar similar to how we did for `AddRecipeView()`, just for consistency.

Okay, now it's time to see it all in action; fire up the iOS simulator and click on the new map icon on the left-hand side of the navigation bar. All going well, it should look a little something like this:

Now go ahead and click on one of the annotations. It should look a little something like this:

Looking good! Now let's go one step further and add a button to our annotation that, when clicked, will dismiss our view and pass back the selected country to our `ContentView()` so our list can be dynamically filtered.

Adding an annotation callout accessory and filtering

In the previous part, we implemented our custom annotations to our `MapView` based on our own actual recipe data. Next, we're going to go a step further and add a button to our annotation (called an **annotation callout accessory**) so that when we click the button, our `MapView` will dismiss and our `ContentView()` will filter recipes by that particular country!

First, however, we need to make a little change to how we get recipes from our `@EnvironmentObject`. Head on over to `ContentView.swift` and add in the following function to our `AppData()` class:

```
func getRecipes(filter: String) -> [RecipeModel] .{
  if filter != "" {
    return recipes.filter ({ $0.origin == filter })
  } else {
    return recipes
  }
}
```

As you can see from the preceding code, we've created a computed property much like our `getFavourites` function, which passes in a parameter of `String`.

It's pretty obvious what we are prepping to do here, but we'll see this in action a little later on.

Next, let's make a change to our `MapKitHelper()`; head on over to `MapKitHelper.swift` and add in the following two variables at the top of our class:

```
@Binding var presentationMode: PresentationMode
@Binding var filter: String
```

We're creating a `@Binding` to `PresentationMode` again – much as we did for our `AddRecipeView()`, we want our `MapKitHelper()` to be able to dismiss our `MapView()` once the callout accessory button is clicked.

Next, we're creating a second `@Binding` to a variable called `filter`. When our callout accessory button is clicked, we'll assign a value to this, which will match our `RecipeModel().origin` property. With this `@Binding`, we can pass this value back through our Views to our `ContentView()` where we'll finally amend our `Helper.getRecipes()` function to filter by `RecipeModel().origin`.

Next, head on down to our `MapViewCoordinator()` class. We'll need to add another `MKMapViewDelegate` called `calloutAccessoryControlTapped` in here:

```
func mapView(_ mapView: MKMapView, annotationView view: MKAnnotationView,
calloutAccessoryControlTapped control: UIControl) {

  parent.filter = (view.annotation?.title ?? "") ?? ""
  parent.presentationMode.dismiss()

}
```

This delegate gets called whenever a `UIControl` item (`UIButton`, in our case) is tapped from inside a callout accessory.

As you can see from the code, we're also doing a bit of logic here. First, we assign our `@Binding` variable, `filter`, the value of our annotation title (which we know to be our `RecipeModel().origin`), then we perform a `.dismiss` on our `PresentationMode` variable.

As both variables are `@Binding`, their parent `@State` values will update accordingly, initially forcing the `RecipeMapView()` sheet to be dismissed. We'll see a little later on how the `filter` binding fits into all this.

Next, still inside `MapKitHelper.swift,` move back to our
other `MKMapViewDelegate-viewFor` annotation and make the following highlighted
amendments:

```
func mapView(_ mapView: MKMapView, viewFor annotation: MKAnnotation) ->
MKAnnotationView? {
   let annotationView = MKAnnotationView(annotation: annotation,
reuseIdentifier: "customView")
   annotationView.canShowCallout = true
   annotationView.image = UIImage(systemName: "book.fill")
   let btn = UIButton(type: .infoDark)
   annotationView.rightCalloutAccessoryView = btn
   return annotationView
}
```

Here, we've added code to create a button of type `.infoDark` (basically a circle with an 'i'
in it) and assigned this to the `rightCalloutAccessoryView` on our `MKAnnotationView`.
And yes, you guessed it, there is a `leftCalloutAccessoryView` too; I'll leave it up to you
to choose which one to use.

Now head on over to `RecipeMapView.swift` and let's make a couple of changes there.
Add in the following variables at the top of our struct:

```
@Binding var filter: String
@Environment(\.presentationMode) var presentationMode
```

We've added the `presentationMode`, which we'll now pass into our `MapView()`.
Remember that we're adding this so that our `MapView` and its
`MapViewCoordinator` delegates can dismiss `RecipeMapView()`.

The other variable we've added is `filter`, but do you notice something a little different?

That's right – normally, you'd expect to see this as a `@State` in order to change the state of
our **RecipeMapView()**, but as we don't want anything to change here (as we're actually
dismissing it), we want this value to be passed back up the stack a little further, right back
to `ContentView()`, as it's here where we will apply the filter.

Before we head on over to `ContentView()`, we need to make the following highlighted
change to the call to `MapView()` from inside `RecipeMapView()`:

```
var body: some View {

   NavigationView {
     MapView(lat: latitude,
        lon: longitude,
```

```
            annotations: Helper.getRecipeLocations(),
            presentationMode: presentationMode,
            filter: $filter)
        .navigationBarTitle(Text("Recipes of the World!"))
    }
}
```

We're done here for now. Let's head back up and over to ContentView.swift and make the following highlighted change:

```
@State private var showAddRecipe = false
@State private var showMap = false
@State private var filter: String = ""
var body: some View { ...
```

Finally, we're able to add in the @State variable for our filters—once this is passed back up to ContentView(), we can use this to filter out specific recipes for that particular country.

Recall the change we made earlier to @EnvironmentObject to pass in the filter parameter to a new computed property we created. We can now use our @State filter here to pass it in.

Make the following highlighted change:

```
if viewIndex == 0 {
  List(appData.getRecipes(filter: filter), id: \.id) { recipe in
    NavigationLink(destination: RecipeDetailView(recipe: recipe)) {
      RecipeView(recipe: recipe)
        .navigationBarTitle(Text("Recipes"))
    }
  }
}
```

Just a small amendment is for us to do by passing in our filter variable to our existing Helper.getRecipes() - then we're pretty much done. Fire up the app in the iOS simulator, navigate to MapView, and select one of our annotations. You should now see our callout accessory button as follows:

Nice! Now go ahead and click on it. All going well, our `RecipeMapView()` should be dismissed and our `ContentView()` should update to show only recipes for the country!

The problem we have now is that we have no way of resetting the filter, but that's an easy fix, so let's do that now.

Adding a reset filter button

Still in `ContentView.swift`, locate the navigation bar button items we created earlier. Remember how we added an `HStack` on the leading button for later? Well, this is *later*, so add in the following highlighted changes to add another button to our leading items:

```
.navigationBarItems(leading: HStack {
  Button(action: {
    self.showMap.toggle()
  }) {
  Image(systemName: "map")
    .renderingMode(.original)
  }.sheet(isPresented: $showMap) {
    RecipeMapView(filter: self.$filter)
  }
  Button(action: {
    self.filter = ""
  }) {
    Image(systemName: "line.horizontal.3.decrease.circle")
      .renderingMode(.original)
  }
  }, trailing:
  Button(action: {
    self.showAddRecipe.toggle()
  }) {
    Image(systemName: "plus")
    .renderingMode(.original)
  }.sheet(isPresented: $showAddRecipe) {
    AddRecipeView().environmentObject(self.appData)
  })
```

Here we've added another `Button` view, which when clicked sets our `filter` variable to an empty string, thereby causing a reload of our SwiftUI View (because it's a `@State` variable).

Go on and give it a try – launch the simulator and filter by country as you did before. Once you've done that, hit the button we've just created and all recipes should return as normal.

Summary

In this chapter, we started by integrating a basic MapKit View into SwiftUI, making use of the `UIViewRepresentable` protocol we picked up in `Chapter 7`, *Creating a Form with States and Data Binding*.

From there, we learned how to add annotations to our map using mock data we created in our `Helper` class. Starting with the basic annotations offered to us by the Apple MapKit framework, we customized our annotations by adding data that was made visible to users when they selected a specific location.

Next, we touched on Apple's Core Location framework by implementing our own `MapLocationManager` and using Xcode to simulate multiple locations from within our app. We saw how SwiftUI updated our `MapView` instantly once our location changed.

Finally, we tied everything together by adding another bar button item to our `ContentView()` that presented our `RecipeMapView()` as a sheet. We then updated and customized our annotations further by displaying how many recipes the selected country had.

We then wrapped it all up by adding a button to our annotations that dismissed our `RecipeMapView()` and filtered our current `ContentView()` list of recipes based on the country selected.

In the next chapter, we'll extend our code base to support the iPad, learning how we can use specific controls in SwiftUI to work seamlessly between iOS and iPadOS.

Questions

1. Which representable protocol will we need to implement MapKit?
2. How do we view our Live map in the Automatic Preview Canvas?
3. Which three properties are required for our `MKAnnotation` subclass?
4. Which framework helped us implement our `MapLocationManager` for notifying changes to our location?
5. What plist key do we need to set when requesting a user's location?

Further reading

- **MapKit:** https://developer.apple.com/documentation/mapkit/mkmapview
- **CoreLocation:** https://developer.apple.com/documentation/corelocation/

10
Updating for iPad with NavigationViewStyle

The iPad has changed the way we use portable computers; with more versatile options becoming available, there is an iPad out there for everyone. This makes it much more important than ever to make sure your app supports the iPad to the best of its (or your) ability.

In this chapter, we'll cover various corners, starting by understanding how an iPad fits into our current project. We'll then move on to the *little things* we can do in preparation for supporting the iPad from the start.

We'll then get to run our app in the iPad simulator and learn about the various layouts that are available to us not only in terms of orientation but the architecture within our code base.

The following topics will be covered in this chapter:

- Updating our project for iPad
- Running our app on iPad for the first time
- Making better use of `NavigationViewStyle`

Technical requirements

For this chapter, you'll need to download Xcode version 11.3 or above from Apple's App Store. You'll also need to be running the latest version of macOS (Catalina or above).

Simply search `Xcode` in the App Store and select and download the latest version.

Launch Xcode and follow any additional installation instructions that your system may prompt you with. Once Xcode has fully launched, you're ready to go.

Updating our project for iPad

Unless you're specifically developing an iPad app, the chances are that you'll always start working on the iPhone version first. Don't worry—we all do it. But working on the iPad version isn't as daunting as you might think, especially as Apple allows you to submit one binary for both platforms.

In this section, we're going to touch on some changes we can make to prep our project to support iPadOS—whether you choose to do this at the start of your project or halfway through, it's worth bearing some of these in mind.

Project settings

Probably one of the easiest things you can do in order to get your app up and running ready for iPadOS is done with a simple checkbox.

If you highlight your project name in the file tree on the left-hand side, then select **General** from the tabs available, you should see the following checkboxes:

If it isn't already, just check **iPad** and your app is ready for launch as an iPad application—it really is that simple.

If you toggle the **iPad** setting off and on, you'll notice that the following two checkboxes appear when **iPad** is selected:

- **Requires full screen**: This is generally for iPad apps that only support one orientation (such as games). Setting this and supporting both orientations is allowed but will most likely fail validation or face rejection from Apple when submitted to the App Store.

- **Supports multiple windows**: This option enables multi-window support. Basically, you can run two versions of your app side by side, such as multiple recipes.

Portrait and landscape support

With the introduction of the Apple Smart Keyboard, it's more important than ever to support multiple orientations on your iPadOS app.

Unless your app specifically requires you to support a set orientation (again, like a game), then there's no excuse really—if you're ever in doubt, just ask yourself whether your app requires a user to input using the keyboard. If so, then support landscape, and if you're supporting landscape for this reason, you should already be supporting portrait.

Regardless making the change to lock orientation for your app is simple.

Again, if you highlight your project name in the file tree on the left-hand side, then select **General** from the tabs available, you should see the following checkboxes:

These options are ticked by default and can be amended as easily as ticking/unticking the ones you require, but there is one slight catch—these aren't device-specific; making these changes will apply to both iOS and iPadOS.

Now, with regard to our recipe app, ideally, we'd be happy with just portrait for iOS, yet would want to support both orientations for iPadOS. For now, make the following changes so we can apply these to all devices:

Go ahead and run the app in the iOS simulator. Once launched, do the following—from the menu bar, click **Hardware | Rotate Left**; you should now see the following:

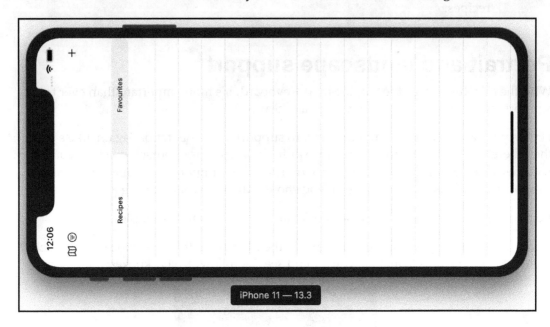

To change this back, simply access the menu bar again and click **Hardware | Rotate Right.**

So, let's now make the change specifically for our app. Head on back over to Info.plist—remember, we visited this in Chapter 9, *Maps and Location Services*, in order to add the permissions message in for our Location Services.

If you take a look at the list, you'll see a key called 'Supported interface orientations (iPad)' already exists. By default, Xcode will automatically assume that you'll want to support rotation for iPad even if you've unticked it in the **General** menu.

If you expand the key, you should see something like the following:

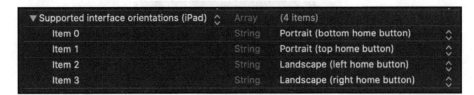

Add and remove these values as you see fit for your app in order to support your desired orientation support—for now, we'll leave these just as they are.

Understanding assets

With iPad support, you'll need to think a little about your assets (images). Choose an image that's big and that looks good on the iPad and you risk the compression of your image on smaller devices and also bloating your app unnecessarily.

Choose images that are too small—that might look great on the phone—and they could be susceptible to stretching and start to look grainy and gain artifacts on your iPad.

Around 90% of the time, you can try to find a happy-medium file in size and in resolution. But for the other 10% of the time, you'll need to work around this.

The common approach is to have iPad-specific images in your Assets.xcassets catalog, as I've done here with the **placeholder-add-image** screenshot:

We can then programmatically choose the image we require based on what device our code is being executed on. For example, the following snippet would allow us to choose the iPad version of our image when running on an iPad:

```
var placeHolderImageName: String {
    return UIDevice.current.userInterfaceIdiom == .pad ? "placeholder-add-
image_iPad" : "placeholder-add-image"
}
```

This computed property will work really well, however, replace every image in your app with two variations and it's going to bloat—fast!

In order to stop this from happening, highlight one of the images from within the Assets.xcassets catalog (either the iPad or the iPhone version), then expand the Inspector window by clicking on the highlighted icon here (situated in the top-right corner of Xcode):

Once that's selected and open, click on the Attributes Inspector (the furthest option on the right), again within the Inspector window:

In here, there are a plethora of options we can change in order to manipulate how our images are rendered within our app. We're not going to cover all of these as it's slightly out of scope for this book, but I'd like you to pay attention to the following options:

As you can see from the preceding screenshot, **Universal** is selected. This means the image will be used for all devices that your app supports.

By highlighting each image and selecting the desired device, we can now start to *thin* down the size of our app.

App thinning (as it's called by Apple) is done automatically and will only build and compile assets into the downloadable binary required for that specific device.

For more information on app thinning and how you reduce the size of your app, see this video from WWDC 2015, where Apple engineers go into it in much more detail: `https://developer.apple.com/videos/play/wwdc2015/404/`.

It might not seem a lot, but small things such as managing your assets correctly can make a big difference when developing an app, and if you start off with these things in mind, as your app grows it will make the whole journey much more manageable.

iPadOS simulators

When the time comes, testing your iPad app is as simple as it is for iOS. If you've set the app to support iPad, you'll be presented with multiple options based on the current version of Xcode you have installed. For example, in Xcode 11.3, you should see the following options:

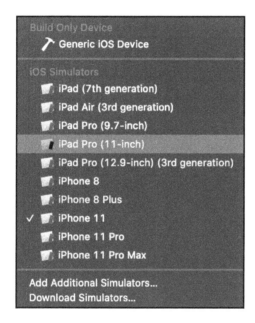

As you can see, we've got five available iPads in our simulator. By default, these will be running iOS 13. This is due to us working with SwiftUI, which requires us to target devices running iOS.

Should we, however, need to test our app with a much earlier version of iOS, we can download all currently supported devices and their versions of iOS. Simply select **Download Simulators...** from the preceding list and you'll be presented with the following:

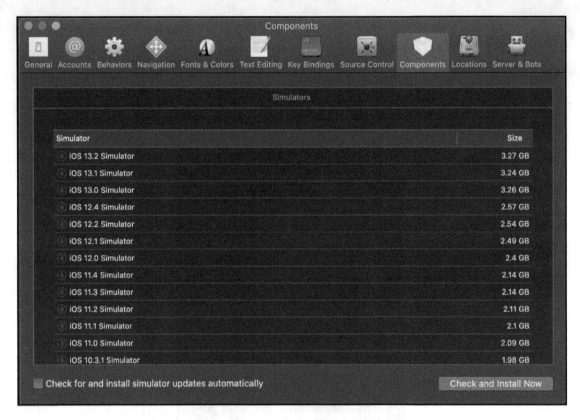

As mentioned before, we are developing our app in SwiftUI, so our app won't work on earlier versions of iOS—so we won't need to download any for this book.

In this section, we outlined some of the *little things* to think about when preparing our app for iPadOS support, such as project settings, how to enable and disable rotation, how to deal with images in the best possible way, and simulators.

In the next section, we'll finally fire up our app on the iPad simulator and see how it all looks, and start to identify some of the areas that may need our attention.

Running our app on iPad for the first time

From what we learned in the previous section, actually getting our app ready for iPad isn't such a daunting task as you may have initially thought it was.

With our project set up, and our orientation ready, and armed with some knowledge about how to fire it up, we'll now start by seeing what exactly is presented to us when we run the simulator.

Running on the simulator

First, let's start by choosing a device from our device list. Any iOS 13 supported device will do, but for the remainder of this book, I'll choose **iPad Pro (11-inch)**:

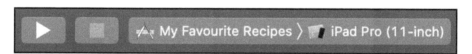

Now you're all set. Just press the *play* button or use the *command + R* keyboard shortcut. The first run of the simulator always takes a little longer than usual (no more than a minute or so, though).

One thing you might notice, especially if you are working on a MacBook, is that the iPad simulator can be a little on the *large* side—as with the iOS simulator, you can resize this manually by moving your cursor to one of the corners and dragging the size down.

Once launched, you should see our app in all its glory. Notice anything wrong, though?

That's right—we're presented with a blank screen. This is due to the way SwiftUI interprets navigation and lists on the iPad in portrait mode. Don't worry—all your hard work is still there and you're still doing a great job.

In fact, switch the simulator to landscape mode and let's see what happens:

There we go—our missing app. It was there all the time! What has happened here is that the way iPad interprets a `ListView` in SwiftUI means that it expected there to be a master (or a detail) page for each item in the list, and by default, without any configuration, iPadOS only supports this in landscape mode.

Let's take a look at how we can fix that in the next section.

Initial support for list views

Start by returning the simulator to portrait mode and then head on over to
`ContentView.swift`. We want to add the following modifier to our `NavigationView`:

```
.navigationViewStyle(StackNavigationViewStyle())
```

Setting `navigationViewStyle` to `StackNavigationViewStyle()` will tell our app to
support `ContentView` by a view stack that only shows a single *top* view at a time,
according to Apple's official SDK documentation.

Go ahead and rerun the simulator. You should see things start to look a little more as we
would expect now:

With that change made, let's see how the rest of our app runs. Go ahead and click on a recipe (or add one in if you've not already done so).

Notice anything odd again? You should see something like the following:

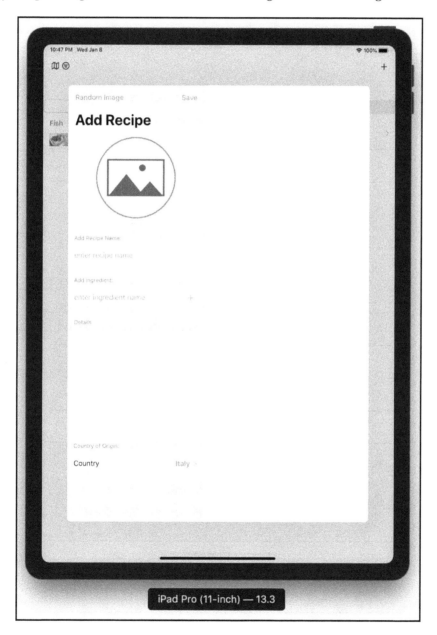

Ahh, broken again... But don't worry—it's a simple fix. Just add in our modifier again and all should be fine. You'll also need to do the same for our `RecipeMapView()` too.

Make the changes and relaunch the simulator. The app should be fully functional now:

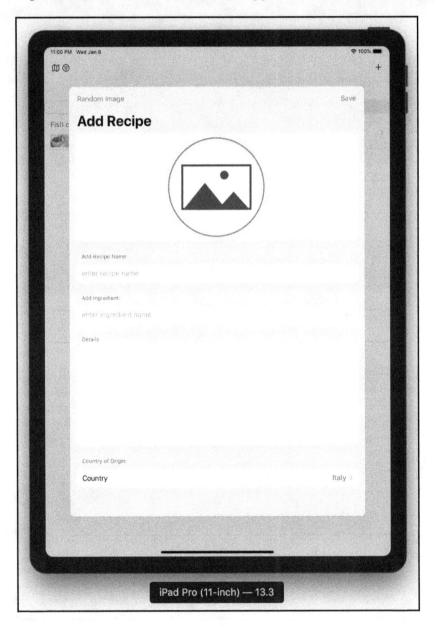

Native components such as `UIImagePickerController()` will automatically adjust to iPadOS, as will any of MapKit's native controls (just not necessarily the SwiftUI view we wrapped it in).

Go ahead and have a play. Try testing your app in various orientations too. You'll find that with SwiftUI there no need (or very little) to adjust our app to support both portrait and landscape, especially if you are using native iOS controls.

In this section, we took our first look at what our app would look like on the iPad, we learned about how the list views created previously are initially interpreted on iPadOS, and we learned how, with a simple modification, we can fix the app and make it usable.

In the next section, we'll dive a little deeper into the `NavigationViewStyle` API and see how we can further enhance the experience, specifically for the iPad.

Making better use of NavigationViewStyle

As we saw earlier in this chapter, supporting iPadOS is now a default option when creating your app project, and most developers (unless specifically told otherwise) will quite happily leave this option ticked.

Sometimes developers get lucky and the iPad version of their app just works—others take the time to completely redesign an iPad-specific version of the app and submit this separately to the App Store. But more often than not, there will be an iPadOS version of your app that is not so much broken but a little *unloved*.

In this section, we'll show you how with SwiftUI and a little bit of upfront thought, you can support iPadOS almost out of the box.

Other NavigationViewStyle options

In the previous section, we saw how adding a `NavigationViewStyle` modifier allowed us to use our iPad app as we first expected.

NavigationViewStyle has three styles we can set for it. Let's take a look and explore the available options:

```
struct DefaultNavigationViewStyle
struct StackNavigationViewStyle
struct DoubleColumnNavigationViewStyle
```

- DefaultNavigationViewStyle is the default that you saw when the iPad app first launched—you'll always be given the default as a selectable option regardless of whether it's the default or not.
- StackNavigationViewStyle is the change we initially made in the previous section, basically disregarding the default behavior for how iPadOS in SwiftUI interprets list views and displaying the app as we see it in the iOS simulator.
- DoubleColumnNavigationViewStyle changes things up a little—we'll be using this in the next section. This is the equivalent to SplitViewController in UIKit—essentially utilizing the size of the iPad's screen to split our list view to the left and a detail view to the right.

DoubleColumnNavigationViewStyle is one of the little things that we can do early on in order to make our transition to iPadOS a little more seamless. The beauty of DoubleColumnNavigationViewStyle is that it won't affect how our app runs on iOS.

Making use of DoubleColumnNavigationViewStyle

As mentioned in the previous section, DoubleColumnNavigationViewStyle for our particular style of app will serve as the best option and make the best use of what SwiftUI has to offer for iPadOS.

Let's start by taking a look at exactly what this will do for us. Head on over to ContentView.swift and change our previously added .navigationViewStyle modifier to the following:

```
.navigationViewStyle(DoubleColumnNavigationViewStyle())
```

Now, if not already done, press resume and check out the automatic preview canvas—notice something different? That's right—because we've selected an iPad device in our device list, our canvas has automatically changed to an iPad layout and, with any luck, you should now see the following:

Let's take a look at how this runs. Run the simulator and add a few recipes if your list is empty.

Now run the simulator again and you should see something odd... That's right—a blank screen. Well, don't worry—that's perfectly normal in portrait mode because of the way we handle iPad list views inside a navigation; simply swipe out from the left-hand bezel and you'll see that the list view magically appears!

Looking good—but what's with all the white space on the right-hand side? Well click on a couple of recipes and let's find out:

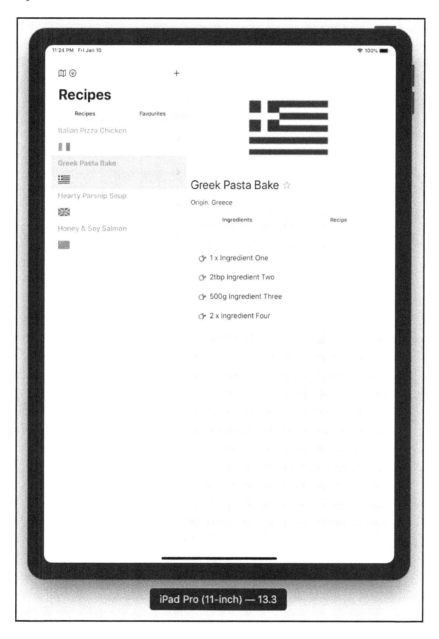

There we have it—as we've set our `NavigationStyleView` to be `DoubleColumnNavigationViewStyle`, SwiftUI has identified that our list contains `NavigationLink` for each of our list view items, thereby displaying our `RecipeDetailView()` in the right-hand column.

Let's have a look and see how things run on the iPhone. Choose an iPhone from the device list and run the app:

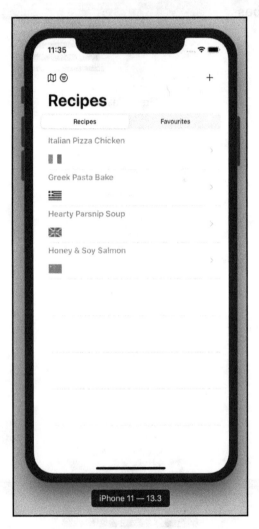

Looks perfect—like nothing's changed! With that all done, we can now look at how to use `DoubleColumnNavigationViewStyle` to improve the architecture of our app.

Improving our architecture with DoubleColumnNavigationViewStyle

With the preceding in mind, let's see how we can improve the architecture of our app. First, we are going to start by renaming our `ContentView.swift` struct. To do this, go to the declaration of the struct, hover over it and secondary-click with your cursor; you should be presented with the following menu:

Click on **Rename** and the renaming tool should automatically launch within Xcode. This will generate a list of references that currently use `ContentView` ready for renaming.

Simply start typing `ListView` and press the *Enter* key once you're done. Xcode will not only rename all references but also rename the file. If you look in the file tree, you should now see `ListView.swift`:

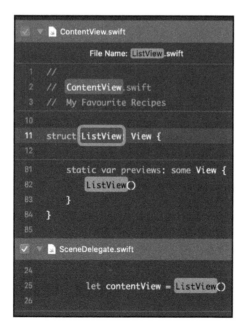

Before we continue with our refactoring, we'll need to make a couple of quick changes in our updated `ContentView.swift` (now called `ListView.swift`). As part of the refactoring, Xcode won't rename the `PreviewProvider` struct we have; make the following highlighted change:

```
struct ListView_Previews: PreviewProvider {
    static var previews: some View {
        ListView()
    }
}
```

All we are doing here is keeping the naming conventions inline, but there is another reason why I've done this, which we'll see shortly.

Next, head on over to `SceneDelegate.Swift`. Here, we're going to need to revert a change made by the refactoring we've just done.

Initially, our root view was set as `ContentView()`—which we refactored to `ListView()`. Well, we no longer want `ListView()` to be our root view, so revert this to `ContentView()`:

```
let appData = AppData()

let contentView = ContentView()

// Use a UIHostingController as window root view controller.
if let windowScene = scene as? UIWindowScene {
```

But wait a minute, did we just get rid of `ContentView.swift`? That's right, but let's bring it back again.

We'll create a new file in our Xcode project called `ContentView` by highlighting the group name in the file tree, right-clicking, and selecting **New File**. Select **SwiftUI View** from the **User Interface** options and click **Next**. Call your new file `ContentView.swift` and click **Create.**

In here, let's add the following highlighted code:

```
struct ContentView: View {
    var body: some View {
        NavigationView {
            ListView()
            WelcomeView()
        }.navigationViewStyle(DoubleColumnNavigationViewStyle())
    }
}
```

Here, we've created `NavigationView` with a modifier of `DoubleColumnNavigationViewStyle`—within the navigation, we've added our new `ListView()` (previously our `ContentView()`) and a new view called `WelcomeView()`. For now, head on over to the file tree and create a basic SwiftUI file called `WelcomeView.swift`.

Don't worry—all will be revealed shortly. What we are doing here, though, is telling our navigation stack that, with `DoubleColumnNavigationViewStyle`, we want to utilize two views. The first will be our `ListView()` and the second will be our `WelcomeView()`.

Once we select an item from our `ListView()`, the `WelcomeView()` will be overwritten with the `RecipeDetailView()` we've selected.

Cleaner navigation architecture

Another benefit to this approach that is that we can house most of our navigation logic inside our `ContentView()`, away from our other views. In fact, we can actually remove a lot of the NavigationViews we used previously and tidy up our code a little.

First, we'll start by bringing `NavigationBarButtonItems` into `ContentView()`. Make the following highlighted changes:

```
ListView(filter: $filter, showAddRecipe: $showAddRecipe)
    .navigationBarTitle(Text(""), displayMode: .inline) // Hack!
    .navigationBarItems(leading: HStack {
    Button(action: {
        self.showMap.toggle()
    }) {
    Image(systemName: "map")
        .renderingMode(.original)
    }.sheet(isPresented: $showMap) {
        RecipeMapView(filter: self.$filter)
    }
    Button(action: {
        self.filter = ""
    }) {
    Image(systemName: "line.horizontal.3.decrease.circle")
        .renderingMode(.original)
    }
    }, trailing:
    Button(action: {
        self.showAddRecipe.toggle()
    }) {
    Image(systemName: "plus")
```

```
        .renderingMode(.original)
    }.sheet(isPresented: $showAddRecipe) {
        AddRecipeView()
    })
```

Here, we've basically taken the contents of `NavigationBarItems` and inserted them into our `ContentView()`. Note that these have been added underneath our `ListView()` and not our new `WelcomeView()`. This is so our bar items can be associated with our `ListView()` and not our `WelcomeView()`.

Also note that we've added a couple of parameters to our `ListView`. We'll need to pass down the filter for our logic to *filter* by country when selected from our `RecipeMapView()`. We're also passing in `showAddRecipe`. This is so our `ListView()` knows to refresh once `AddRecipeDetails()` has been dismissed (again, using two-way binding).

Now we need to head on over to `ListView.swift`. Make the following highlighted changes in here:

```
@State private var viewIndex = 0
@Binding var filter: String
@Binding var showAddRecipe: Bool
var body: some View {
```

First, we'll start by amending the preceding variables from `private` to `public`. We'll then amend the prefix to `@Binding` as we'll be listening to changes from our `ContentView()`.

Next, we'll strip away any reference to `NavigationView` from in here, as we'll no longer need this. Have a go—the inside of our body view should look something like the following:

```
VStack {
    Picker(selection: $viewIndex, label: Text("")) {
        Text("All").tag(0)
        Text("Favourites").tag(1)
    }.pickerStyle(SegmentedPickerStyle())
    if viewIndex == 0 {
        List(appData.recipes, id: \.id) { recipe in
            NavigationLink(destination: RecipeDetailView(recipe: recipe)) {
                RecipeView(recipe: recipe)
            }
        }
    } else if viewIndex == 1 {
        List(appData.favourites, id: \.id) { recipe in
            NavigationLink(destination: RecipeDetailView(recipe: recipe)) {
                RecipeView(recipe: recipe)
            }
```

```
            }
        }
    }
```

Now let's tidy up some more code. Head on over to `RecipeMapView.swift`, remove `NavigationView` from in there, and add a `Text()` view to the top of the page to give it a title:

```
VStack {
    Text("Recipes of the World!")
        .font(.headline)
        .padding()
        .multilineTextAlignment(.leading)
    MapView(lat: latitude,
            lon: longitude,
            annotations: Helper.getRecipeLocations(),
            presentationMode: presentationMode,
            filter: $filter)
}
```

Do the same over at `AddRecipeView.swift` too, but by removing `NavigationView()`, you'll need to make a slight tweak in order to keep the functionality—have a go by adding some buttons to the form view we already created. If you get stuck, have a look at the sample code and see how I did it.

Final check on our iPhone and iPad app

Well, we're almost done—just one last thing to do now, and that's to run over our functionality for both iPhone and iPad.

Start by launching the simulator for iOS and navigate around. Note that, since the last time we launched in iPhone mode, nothing has really changed. The only thing you should see is that iPhones don't actually make use of our new `WelcomeView()`.

This is mainly due to the fact that our iPhone view doesn't really need one; the smaller screen size houses the `ListView()` well and it doesn't look out of place.

Now go ahead and launch the app on the iPad in portrait mode. Imagine our `ListView()` as we saw earlier—looking all lost in that big space. Now we can design a welcome screen that could potentially have details on how to use the app or some additional recipe tips and tricks (basically, anything you want).

If you swipe out from the left-hand bezel to the right-hand one, you'll see our `ListView()` appear, looking nice and formatted and not out of place at all. Tap on one of the items and the `WelcomeView()` transforms into our `RecipeDetailView()`.

In this section, we took everything we learned about how our app works on an iPad and cleaned up our code and `NavigationView` architecture. We now understand how the iPad, both in portrait and landscape mode, interprets a list within a navigation and the changes we can make to this universally on both iOS and iPadOS.

Summary

In this chapter, we learned everything we needed to know about iPad and iPadOS. We learned that if we make some good decisions early on, supporting the iPad isn't going to be such a big chore as we might think.

We looked at handling assets and best practices to stop our binaries from being bloated. We saw how to support different orientations based on our users' needs and the changes we need to make to our `info.plist` to support these.

Next, we looked at what our iPad app would look like straight out of the box—we launched the app in the iPad simulator to see how our iPhone design looked so far. We then made use of `NavigationView` in order to support the split view designed specifically for iPad yet without compromising our iPhone app.

In the next chapter, we'll move away from our main devices and take to our wrists as we develop an Apple Watch companion app for our Recipe app.

Questions

1. Where would we overwrite specific orientation support for just an iPad?
2. Which window would we find the checkbox to support an image just for iPad in?
3. How do we test our iPad app through Xcode (two answers here)?
4. How many types of NavigationViewStyle are there? Can you name them all?
5. Which NavigationViewStyle do we use for iPad split-screen support?

Further reading

- **App Thinning:** `https://developer.apple.com/videos/play/wwdc2015/404/`

11
SwiftUI on watchOS

Welcome to Chapter 11! In this chapter, we are going to create our very own Apple Watch Companion app. For our iOS recipe app, we'll start by covering how we actually develop for watchOS and how Xcode interprets our Watch App within our current project.

We'll then create our Watch project and see how we can integrate it with our current project, reusing some of our existing code.

After that comes the good stuff. We'll look at how we can use the power of SwiftUI to easily create multiple watch interfaces with just a couple of lines of code and by dropping in with ease familiar syntax we've used earlier.

Finally, we'll hook up our iOS app and Watch App, and send newly created recipes straight over to our watch so that we can check our ingredients on the go.

The following topics will be covered in this chapter:

- Developing for watchOS
- Creating a watchOS project
- Using SwiftUI to create a list of recipes
- Passing data between our App and watchOS

Technical requirements

For this chapter, you'll need to download Xcode version 11.3 or above from the Apple Mac App Store. You'll also need to be running the latest version of macOS (Catalina or above).

Simply search for Xcode in the App Store, and select and download the latest version.

Launch Xcode and follow any additional installation instructions that your system may prompt you for. Once Xcode has fully launched, you're ready to go.

Developing for watchOS

Announced back in 2015, watchOS and Apple Watch was the most anticipated wearable to be released by Apple. With a Developer SDK straight from the word go, App Store apps could now allow users to have a companion in the form of an extension right on their wrists.

In this section, we'll delve a little into the understanding of how we start to develop for watchOS within our current Xcode project with the use of extensions. We'll learn a little about the history of watchOS and where it all started for developers.

Let's get started by understanding a little more about the watchOS framework, **WatchKit**.

What is WatchKit?

WatchKit is the framework developed by Apple that is used by developers to create watchOS apps. Unveiled at WWDC 2015 alongside Xcode 7 beta, developers were given the power to create companion apps that would run alongside their parent apps.

Initially, watchOS apps needed a parent app to work (or exist even), and they were built as an **extension** to the parent iOS project from within Xcode. Recently, watchOS branched off from this approach and with the birth of the App Store for Apple Watch, an independent watchOS app could be built.

For this book, we'll concentrate on building a companion app using iOS extensions as our method to implement this. We'll take a closer look now at what **extensions** are and how they sit within our project.

Understanding extensions

Extensions, particularly in iOS, aren't just for watchOS, they are used for many other components such as Today (widgets), photo sharing, custom keyboard, and audio.

Extensions are designed to allow interaction between the app and another UI element. Take the Today extension, for example —this is an external UI component that sits on your home screen in iOS, yet interacts directly with your app (and from within your app's project in Xcode).

You need to remember that extensions are not a permanent feature of your app, as a user can choose whether or not to interact with the extension or even enable it. Apple's guidelines suggest that when building an extension, think carefully about its design and make sure it looks like it belongs and functions how the user would expect it to.

The same applies to watchOS too, given how a user expects to interact with watchOS (for example, scrolling with the digital crown). User expectations should play a big part in how you think about and design your extension.

Next, let's look specifically at how watchOS works with extensions.

Extensions in watchOS

Although we're going to create a companion watchOS app within our current iOS project, watchOS is still an app in its own right. Apple initially took this approach as a view to eventually creating standalone apps, hence setting a base foundation for developers to build standalone watchOS apps going forward.

The `app` element of our companion (the WatchKit App) is just like we would expect. It has its own `Assets.xcassets` catalog; its own settings file, `info.plist`; and even its own Target so that we can run it as an app. But as we'll see in the next section, no code as such lives there.

The code is created separately in an `Extension` folder, which is specifically generated for the watchOS project. The WatchKit App is responsible only for the scene and interactions (such as buttons), and additional logic and execution are passed off to the extension to handle:

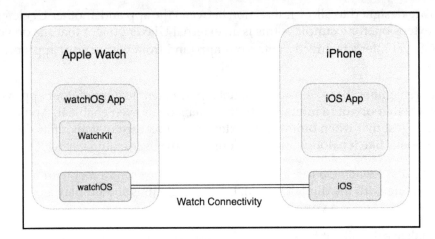

The preceding diagram shows how the WatchKit App interacts with the WatchKit extension.

All of this is great to know and forms a basic understanding of the watchOS architecture, but let's put it into practice. In the next section, we'll take our existing recipe project and start to create our very own watchOS app!

Creating a watchOS project

In this section, we'll start by taking our existing recipe project and through Xcode, we'll go through and, learn how to create a **Watch App for iOS App**.

Once we've done that, we'll take a look at the updated project structure, and, as per the previous section, we'll be able to see in more detail the separation between the **WatchKit App** and the **extension**.

Updating our project

Let's start by heading on over to Xcode and highlighting the project name at the top of the File Tree. With the project tree highlighted, take a look at the column to the right, which contains a list of projects and targets.

At the bottom of the column, you should see a + button. Click on this and you will be presented with an action sheet that says **Choose a template for your new target**.

Here, select **watchOS** from the top list and then select **Watch App for iOS App**:

Then, click on **Next**, where you'll be presented with the options for your next target. You might recognize this from Chapter 4, *Creating Your First Application*. The same principles apply, but we'll go through the two changes we'll need to make:

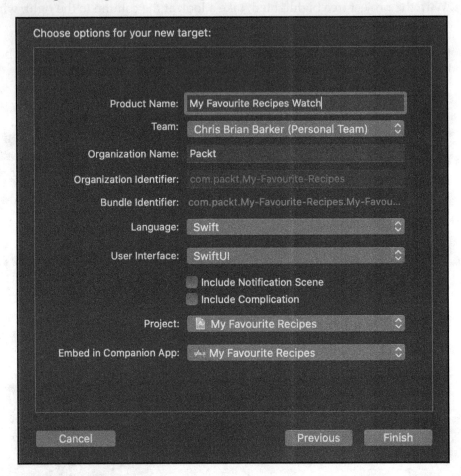

First add a **Product Name**. This can be anything you like; however, remember that this will be initially shown as the name for the app on the watch (although it can be changed later in info.plist if you want).

Next, you'll need to untick **Include Complication** as this is a little out of scope for this book, but, for reference, a complication is the little *widget* you can add to your watch face.

Once we've done that, click **Finish**; you'll then be presented with the following:

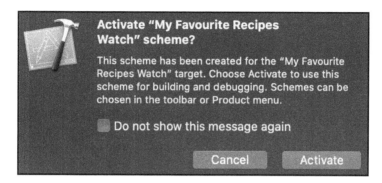

Click **Activate**.

Changes to our project

Now that's all done, let's take a look at the changes that have been made in Xcode. First, you'll see that there have been two additions to our targets:

- **My Favourite Recipes Watch**
- **My Favourite Recipes Watch Extension**

Also, the same two named groups have appeared in our File Tree too:

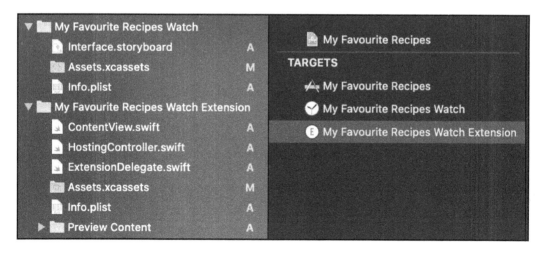

Our **My Favourite Recipes Watch** target is our WatchKit App and the **My Favourite Recipes Watch Extension** is exactly what it says on the tin, the extension element of our Watch App.

Referring back to the content in our previous section, if we take a look at the File Tree, you can see that, under **My Favourite Recipes Watch**, we now have `Interface.storyboard`, `Assets.xcassets`, and `Info.plist`—the basic App elements of our Watch App.

Additionally, if we look under the **My Favourite Recipes Watch Extension** group, you'll see three ***.swift** files created:

- `ContentView.swift`
- `HostingController.swift`
- `ExtensionDelegate.swift` (the watchOS equivalent of `AppDelegate.swift`)

We'll go through these in a moment, but first, let's head back up to the **My Favourite Recipes Watch** group and click on `Interface.storyboard`. You should see the following appear in Xcode's central window:

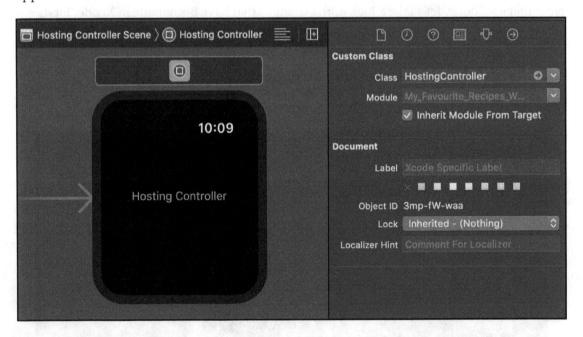

Here, you'll be presented with the storyboard for the watch layout. Initially, this may seem a little old fashioned for SwiftUI (*as storyboards are usually associated as a UIKit thing*), but we'll see now how this all hooks up.

Notice the name of the class already assigned in the Identity Inspector—that's right, it's the `HostingController` class from our generated `HostingController.swift` file.

Currently, watchOS doesn't support SwiftUI directly in the App/UI layer. The way we handle this is to use our `HostingController` class to harness our SwiftUI View and present this to our UI layer. Think back to `Chapter 8`, *Networking and Linking to Your Existing App Logic,* and how we presented our MapKit back to SwiftUI in `MapKitHelper.swift`. Although executed in a slightly simpler way, the same principles apply.

Let's take a look at our `HostingContoller.swift` file to see how this all works:

```
import WatchKit
import Foundation
import SwiftUI

class HostingController: WKHostingController<ContentView> {
    override var body: ContentView {
        return ContentView()
    }
}
```

I've highlighted a couple of areas to pay attention to, but as we can see, we have a class that conforms to `WKHostingController`, which is used to create view controllers in watchOS apps (think UIViewController equivalent).

Notice that when we conform to `WKHostingController`, this is also a type of `ContentView()`. This is `ContentView()`, which has just been created in our **My Favourite Recipes Watch** group. We can now override our body from `ContentView()` and then return the View itself to `Interface.storyboard`.

If we take a look at `ContentView.swift`, we'll soon feel back on familiar ground. This is just our basic SwiftUI View:

```
struct ContentView: View {
    var body: some View {
        Text("Hello, World!")
    }
}

struct ContentView_Previews: PreviewProvider {
    static var previews: some View {
        ContentView()
    }
}
```

And that's the structure of our watchOS app. We'll now go on to add our code in `ContentView.swift` just as we would for any other view.

In the next section, we'll begin to build our watchOS app, looking at how we can use lists that we've previously worked with to display a list of our recipes right on our wrist!

Using SwiftUI to create a list of recipes

We'll start with something simple as more of a proof of concept of how watchOS can harness SwiftUI. We'll also learn how we can reuse some of our classes and models from our parent application.

Creating a List() view in watchOS

Let's start by heading on over to our `ContentView.swift`. Now, remember, that's `ContentView.swift` in our **My Favourite Recipes Watch Extension** group (not our parent app). Make the following highlighted changes:

```
struct ContentView: View {
    var recipes = [RecipeModel]()
    var body: some View {
        VStack {
            Text("Recipes")
                .font(.headline)
            List(recipes, id: \.id) { recipe in
                Text("\(recipe.name)")
            }
        }
    }
}
```

Here, we've started by creating a variable for our recipes. This is an array of `RecipeModel()` from our parent class.

Next, into the body of our struct, we've added some familiar controls: `VStack`, which wraps around `Text()`, and a `List()` view.

Much like our app, the `List()` view iterates around our array of recipes and displays the name in an enclosing `Text()` view.

Now, we'll need to try and build the app. First, we'll need to make sure we've selected our target in the scheme list:

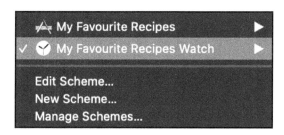

Once selected, press *command + B* to build. Do you notice anything? That's right, we've got some errors. Our `RecipeModel()` is not part of our current watch project. Luckily, this is an easy fix—head on over to `RecipeModel.swift` and highlight the file.

Next, select the **File Inspector** in the right-hand column of Xcode and take note of the **Target Membership** section; notice that our **My Favourite Recipes Watch Extension** is unchecked—check it, and that's it.

If we now build the app, we should see that it all compiles as normal. Bring up the automatic preview windows and click **Resume**, and you'll be presented with an empty watch face with the text **Recipes**.

Using our mock data

With that done, let's inject some mock data into our app. The good news is that we can reuse our `Helper.mockData()` class from our main app; head on over to `Helper.swift` and highlight the file.

We're going to want to include this as part of our **My Favourite Recipes Watch Extension** project, so similar to what we did with `RecipeDetail()`, select the **File Inspector** in the right-hand column of Xcode, take note of the **Target Membership** section, and check **My Favourite Recipes Watch Extension.**

Go ahead and try and press *command + B* to build the app. You'll notice that the following errors are thrown up:

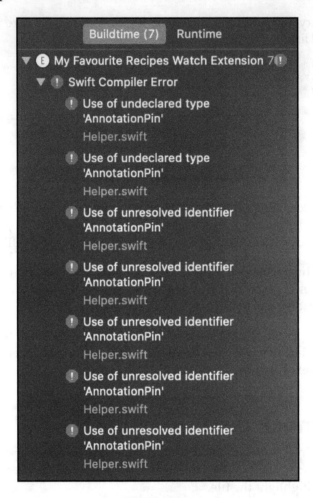

That's because our `Helper` class references the `AnnotationPin()` class, which currently lives inside `MapKitHelper.swift` (which we haven't added to our **My Favourite Recipes Watch Extension** target). Now, I know what you're thinking: we could just go and add this file to our target, but chances are this will lead us down a massive rabbit hole, so our simple solution would be to extract the `AnnotationPin()` class into its own file.

Create a new **Swift File** (you should be familiar with this process by now) and call it
AnnotationPin. Just before you click **Create**, you'll be presented with the following:

Notice here the **Targets** section at the bottom; this is your opportunity when creating new
files to decide which target you want the file to be associated with. By default, our main
project will already be checked, so now just check the **My Favourite Recipes Watch
Extension** target and click **Create**.

Now cut and paste the entire `AnnotationPin()` class from `MapKitHelper.swift` into our new file. Press *command + B* to build and all should be well.

Go back on over to `ContentView.swift` in our **My Favourite Recipes Watch Extension** group and make the following highlighted changes to our preview provider:

```
struct ContentView_Previews: PreviewProvider {
    static var previews: some View {
        ContentView(recipes: Helper.mockRecipes())
    }
}
```

We've simply just added a call to our `Helper.mockRecipes()` function inside the constructor of `ContentView`. Now, go ahead and view the changes in the automatic preview canvas. You should see something like the following:

This is great. Now, let's add a couple more screens to make our Watch App a little more useful.

Multiple screens in watchOS

Back before the days of SwiftUI, to achieve multiple screens, we would need to add additional `HostingController` to our storyboard. But with SwiftUI, we can eliminate this by having just one default `HostingController`, which acts as a harness or entry point for our watchOS app.

To create a new screen, we'll first need to create a new file. Highlight the **My Favourite Recipes Watch Extension** group and create a new Swift UI View file and call it `IngredientsView.swift`.

Once created, add the highlighted code as follows:

```
var ingredients = [String]()
var recipeName = ""
var body: some View {
    VStack {
        Text(recipeName)
            .font(.headline)
        List(ingredients, id: \.self) { ingredient in
            Text(ingredient)
        }
    }
}
```

There's nothing too fancy here; we've created another `List()` view with a `Text()` header of ingredients, and again we have an array of `String()` to hold our list of ingredients for our specific recipe. Have a look in the automatic preview window and you should see a similar result to the previous one we created.

Now, it's time to inject some data. First, head on over to `Helper.swift` and find the `getMockIngredients()` function. A simple change here—just remove `private` from the start of the function to make this a publicly available function.

Now, go back on over to `IngredientsView.swift` and make the following highlighted changes to the preview provider:

```
struct IngredientsView_Previews: PreviewProvider {
    static var previews: some View {
        IngredientsView(ingredients: Helper.getMockIngredients(),
recipeName: "Ingredients")
    }
}
```

Here, much like in `ContentView_Previews`, we're passing on our mock data. Now, check out the automatic preview canvas and you should see something like the following:

There we go—a list of ingredients for our given recipe. Now, let's take a look at how we can bind these together.

Adding multiple screens

With SwiftUI, this is one of the easiest things to implement in watchOS, especially compared to the original way of doing it.

Previously, you would set up a custom segue in your storyboard, then implement a delegate method to detect a tap on a row, and then wrap up the data you wanted to pass over into a dictionary, followed by unwrapping at the other end. It's nothing too difficult—just tedious.

Now, with SwiftUI, we can fix this with one simple little wrapper that you've already seen before. Take a look, and make the following highlighted changes in your `ContentView()` struct:

```
VStack {
    Text("Recipes")
        .font(.headline)
    List(recipes, id: \.id) { recipe in
        NavigationLink(destination: IngredientsView(ingredients:
recipe.ingredients, recipeName: recipe.name)) {
            Text("\(recipe.name)")
        }
```

```
        }
    }
```

Yes, it really is as simple as that. Just wrap `NavigationLink()` around the contents of each `List()` item and you're good to go. Also, we don't even need to add `NavigationView` in SwiftUI for watchOS—this is all handled by the WatchKit framework.

Now that we've seen what our Watch App looks like on the canvas, let's take a look at it running on the simulator—yes, Xcode has simulators for Apple Watch, too.

If you take a look at the device list while you're on the **My Favourite Recipes Watch** target, you'll see a list of Apple Watch simulators to choose from, just like the following:

Choose one (any is fine) and run the app just like you would run the iPhone or iPad app. After a moment or so, you should be presented with the Apple Watch simulator of your choice, but unfortunately, there won't be a lot to see as our Watch App doesn't have any recipe data (and our mock data is only being used for the preview canvas).

Remember, we're building a companion app, so it will rely on data from the main app to display any content. We're going to look at connectivity shortly, but in the meantime, let's do a very quick hack to see how it looks.

Make the following highlighted changes to `ContentView()` and rerun the app:

```
struct ContentView: View {
    //var recipes = [RecipeModel]()
    var recipes: [RecipeModel] = Helper.mockRecipes()
    var body: some View {
```

Here, we've just commented out our original recipe variable and added a new one pointing to our mock data helper. Notice that, when the simulator launches, we now not only have items on our list, but we can also tap on them to display our list of ingredients:

In this section, we've started to build our very own watchOS companion app. We've learned how to take the knowledge and simplicity we learned in previous chapters and create two `ListViews()` that interact with each other with ease.

This looks great! Now let's go one step further and add a little home screen to our app. Again, highlight the **My Favourite Recipes Watch Extension** group and create a new Swift UI View file and call it `HomeView.swift`.

Once created, add the highlighted code as follows:

```
struct HomeView: View {
    var body: some View {
        VStack {
            Text("My Favourite Recipes")
                .font(.callout)
            NavigationLink(destination: ContentView()) {
                Text("Show Recipes")
            }
        }
    }
}
```

Feel free to style the `Text()` view how you see fit with some of the modifiers we've used in previous chapters.

As you can see here, we've created `NavigationLink()` that pushes directly to `ContentView()` (which is our current list of recipes). There's no need for an extra `HostingController` or any additional code—just the straightforward simplicity of SwiftUI.

We will, however, have to make a couple of minor tweaks to our current `HostingController.swift` file. Head on over there now and make the following highlighted changes:

```swift
class HostingController: WKHostingController<HomeView>, WCSessionDelegate {
    override var body: HomeView {
        return HomeView()
    }
}
```

As you can see from the code, we've simply replaced any reference to `ContentView` with `HomeView` as this is now our new entry point for our watchOS app.

Go ahead now and run the watchOS app on the simulator. You should be able to see our new `HomeView()`, with a tap straight through to `ContentView()`:

In this section, we've started to build our very own watchOS app. We've learned how SwiftUI integrates and coexists with the existing `HostingController` framework. We've seen how we can reference classes created in our parent project to be reused in our watchOS app.

Next, we again saw the simplicity that SwiftUI has to offer in terms of creating and accessing new views with our watchOS app.

For the final section of this chapter, we'll take a look at how we can send our own generated recipes straight over to our Watch App by using the `WatchConnectivity` framework so that we can display our list of recipes directly on our wrist.

Passing data between our app and watchOS

In this section, we are going to learn how to pass data from the parent app straight into the watchOS app. We will do this by updating our recipe list on our watch with a recently added recipe from `AddRecipeView()`.

When watchOS first came on the scene, passing data was a little tricky, to say the least. We first had to create an *App Group* that was shared by both the iOS app and the watchOS app. Here, we could persist *shared* `UserDefaults`, which could be accessed by both the parent app and the watch.

 UserDefaults is a lightweight way of storing data in your projects, using a key-value approach. You can easily persist anything from `String`, `Bool`, `Int`, `Array`, or `Data` in your app.

With watchOS 2.0 came `WatchConnectivity`—a new and more effective way of sending data from our iOS app straight to our wrist.

The initial API gave us a function called `WCSession.transferUserInfo`, which allowed us to pass a dictionary to the app while the watchOS wasn't running but, in turn, could not receive data back from the request.

Another function made available was `WCSession.sendMessage`; initially, this call would allow you to receive a message back from the watchOS companion app once the initial message had been received, although early versions of this API would only work if the watchOS was running.

Recent changes to `WCSession.sendMessage` now allow messages to be sent that will wake the watchOS app should it need to. As of February 2020, `WCSession.transferUserInfo` was not marked as deprecated; however, it seems to be unsupported in Xcode 11.3 for its original intended use.

With this in mind, let's start by looking at how we set up `WatchConnectivity` in our SwiftUI app by adding this into our parent app.

Initializing WatchConnectivity in iOS

Let's start by creating a new class in our parent app called `WatchManager.swift`. Inside the class, we are going to make the following changes. I'll break these down a section at a time so we can go through them:

```
import WatchConnectivity

class WatchManager: NSObject, WCSessionDelegate {
    // MARK: - Watch Delegates
    func session(_ session: WCSession, activationDidCompleteWith
activationState: WCSessionActivationState, error: Error?) { }
    func sessionDidBecomeInactive(_ session: WCSession) { }
    func sessionDidDeactivate(_ session: WCSession) { }

    // Remaining code here...

}
```

First, we'll start by telling our class that we want to use the `WatchConnectivity` framework; we do this by adding `importWatchConnectivity` to the top of our class.

Next, we want to make sure we conform to two protocols, `NSObject` and `WCSessionDelegate`. The first is required because we are going to create a shared instance of our class. The next is the delegate method used by our `WatchConnectivty` session (`WCSession`).

By design, Xcode will now prompt us that we currently don't conform to the `WCSessionDelegate` protocol, so we'll add in the preceding three delegate functions to satisfy this. Although required, we won't be making use of these functions for this chapter. But as you can probably tell by the name, they are used to monitor the states of `WCSession`.

Next, let's add in our initializers as highlighted here:

```
class WatchManager: NSObject, WCSessionDelegate {
    // Previous code here...

    static let sharedInstance = WatchManager()
    override init() {
        super.init()
        if WCSession.isSupported() {
```

```
            let session = WCSession.default
            session.delegate = self
            session.activate()
        }
    }
}
```

The first is the static property that we'll use for our shared instance. Basically, once we initialize our class using this shared instance, our app will keep the instance of this alive until the app is shut down.

The second is our basic initializer. First, we check whether WCSession is supported on the current device. If so, we then initialize and activate the session.

Once you've got those initializers, add in the following final functions:

```
func sessionReachabilityDidChange(_ session: WCSession) {
    if !WCSession.default.isReachable {
        WCSession.default.activate()
    }
}
```

The first is an optional delegate (meaning our class is not required to conform to it). This function checks to see whether our companion app is available. If not, it tries to initialize WCSession again. Connectivity with watchOS (especially when debugging in the simulator) can be a little temperamental, so it's a good idea to have this check in place.

Now, add the following final function:

```
func send(recipe: RecipeModel) {
    WCSession.default.sendMessage(["recipe.data": recipe.toJson()],
replyHandler: nil)
}
```

This is our send function, which will grab our recipe data and send it using WCSession.sendMessage over to our watchOS app. Notice here that we are passing a dictionary across. We've given it the key of recipe.data so we can identify this at the watch's end, and we are passing RecipeModel, which we have converted into JSON.

 You'll notice Xcode giving you a compiler warning on the .toJson() function—don't worry, we'll add this on in the next part.

Now, head on over to `AppDelegate.swift` and make the following highlighted change:

```
func application(_ application: UIApplication,
didFinishLaunchingWithOptions launchOptions:
[UIApplication.LaunchOptionsKey: Any]?) -> Bool {
    // Override point for customization after application launch.
    _ = WatchManager.sharedInstance
    return true
}
```

The app delegate is, as some might say, the heart of the app.
The `didFinishLaunchingWithOptions` function is one of the first accessible functions to be called when an app first starts.

Here is where we will kick-start our instance of `WatchManager()`. Making the preceding highlighted change will initialize the class and allow us to access the current `WCSession` from within `WatchManager()`. As long as we call all functions via `sharedInstance`, we'll have access to the same session.

Sending data to watchOS

First, we need to add a couple of small functions to our `RecipeModel()` struct. Head on over to `RecipeModel.swift` and add in the following functions. I suggest you grab them from the example code rather than type them out in full as we only really need to know *what* they do rather than *how* they do it:

```
func toJson() -> String {
    // Get function from Code Sample
}

static func createFrom(json: String) -> RecipeModel {
    // Get function from Code Sample
}
```

The `toJson` function will simply convert `RecipeModel()` into a JSON string that we can add to our `WCSession.sendMessage()` call.

The `createFrom` static function will convert our JSON string back into `RecipeModel()` on the watchOS side.

Next, head on over to `AddRecipeView.swift` and add in the following highlighted code at the end of your `saveRecipe()` function:

```
private func saveRecipe() {
    // Previous code here...

    WatchManager.sharedInstance.send(recipe: newRecipe)
}
```

Here, we are making a call to the `send()` function we created in `WatchManager()`. Notice how we make the call via `sharedInstance`.

And that's pretty much it from the parent app's perspective. We've now got everything in place to send a message and our recipe to our watchOS app.

Next, we'll head on over to our Watch extension to see how we receive the message and add this to `RecipeListView()`.

Receiving data on watchOS

First, let's start by heading on over to `HostingController.swift` and conforming our class to `WCSessionDelegate`.

Before we do anything, we'll need to import the `WatchConnectivity` framework:

```
import WatchConnectivity
```

Now, we can add the `WCSessionDelegate` protocol to our class:

```
class HostingController: WKHostingController<HomeView>, WCSessionDelegate {

    // Remaining code here...
}
```

This will force us to add the following delegate methods into our class:

```
func session(_ session: WCSession, activationDidCompleteWith
activationState: WCSessionActivationState, error: Error?) { }
```

We can leave `activationDidCompleteWith activationState` empty as we won't be needing this for our app. Although, if you wanted to add any error handling, you would do so here.

Next, add our final delegate method, and populate with the following content:

```
func session(_ session: WCSession, didReceiveMessage message: [String :
Any]) {
    if let keyName = message.keys.first,
        let value = message[keyName] as? String {
            recipes = WatchHelper.addRecipe(recipeString: value)
            setNeedsBodyUpdate()
    }
}
```

Here is our delegate that will handle `sendMessage` from the watchOS side of things. In the same way that we sent the message over in `WatchManager()`, we'll receive a dictionary that we can pull out our JSON string from and convert it back into `RecipeModel()`.

You'll also see that we are referencing a `recipes` variable. Let's go ahead and create that to also make a change to our body function:

```
@Published var recipes = WatchHelper.getRecipes()
    override var body: HomeView {
        return HomeView(recipes: recipes)
    }
```

This `@Published` variable will be used to push any changes to our recipe variable. As we are in `HostingController()`, we'll need to push this along a little by using `setNeedsBodyUpdate()` after we've updated our recipe variable.

Once those are in place, we'll need to initialize `WCSession`, much like we did back in `WatchManager()`. As `HostingController()` is our main entry point for the app, we can do this here.

Update the following function with the highlighted code. You'll notice this is nearly identical to what we've added in before:

```
override func willActivate() {
    super.willActivate()
    if WCSession.isSupported() {
        let session = WCSession.default
        session.delegate = self
        session.activate()
    }
}
```

Believe it or not, we're almost ready to roll! We just need to add a couple of helper functions to grab our recipes and convert our JSON into `RecipeModel()`.

Create a new class called `WatchHelper.swift`. You'll find this in the same code. Copy the following functions complete with the code from there, and I'll give you a brief overview of what they are doing (*again, it's not that important for you to know how they work*):

```
class WatchHelper: Any {
    // Add Recipe
    static func addRecipe(recipeString: String) -> [RecipeModel] {
        // Remaing code here...
    }
    static func getRecipes() -> [RecipeModel] {
        // Remaing code here...
    }
}
```

The `addRecipe` function takes our JSON and converts it into `RecipeModel()` using `createFrom()` we added in earlier. We'll also persist this to the watch's UserDefaults so we can grab it later.

Next, `getRecipes` does exactly what it says on the tin—it pulls the list of recipes we've saved from the watch and returns them as an array of `RecipeModel()`.

Right, here comes the crunch; press *command + B* on both targets and, if all is going well, your project and each target should build successfully!

Now, it's time to fire up the simulators and see your great work in action!

Testing sendMessage() end to end

First of all, select the **My Favourite Recipes Watch** target and press command + *R*. Wait for your simulator to launch as normal until you get `HomeView()`:

Next, still with the watch simulator running, go ahead and launch the parent app, then add your favorite recipe as normal and click **Save**.

Give it about 10 seconds (it takes a little while longer in the simulator) and then click **Show Recipes** back on the watch simulator. You should now see the recipe you just added and be able to successfully tap through to your ingredients:

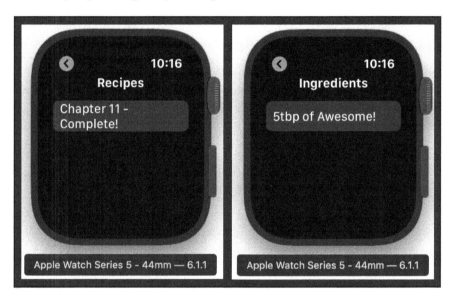

And that's it! Well done! You've now successfully passed data from your recipe app straight over to your watch. Why don't you go ahead and add another screen passing across the recipe instructions and see how you get on.

It's worth noting that WatchConnectivity can be a little *temperamental* in the simulators. Apple recommends always testing on real devices, but for the scope of this book, a quick shutdown and restart of Xcode and both simulators usually do the trick!

In this section, we learned a lot about `WatchConnectivity` and how we handle this from both the parent app and the companion app. We saw how to best initialize and set up `WCSession`, so we can send messages any time to our Watch App, and how to receive them making use of the `sendMessage()` API.

Summary

We started by looking at how Xcode interprets a Watch App within an existing project. From this, we learned about extensions and their file structure when created in Xcode.

Next, we created our Apple Watch project and familiarized ourselves with the autogenerated code; we looked at how the newly created **My Favourite Recipes Watch** target now offers us Apple Watch simulators that we can use in the same way as iOS or iPadOS simulators.

When we finally got stuck into developing our Watch App, we saw how `HostingController` acts as an entry point for our watchOS app, harnessing our initial SwiftUI View, hence allowing us to create simple `List()` views and `Text()` views, just like we had done previously.

We were then introduced to the `WatchConnectivity` framework. We learned about the APIs available to us for communicating and sending direct messages from our parent app to our Watch App. With this, we hooked them up together and successfully sent a recipe from our app to our watch.

Finally, we looked at how we can make use of the watchOS and iOS simulators not only to test our newly created watchOS app but to send data to and from both iOS and watchOS simulators.

In the next chapter, we'll go back over our app and take a look at what we've learned with SwiftUI and compare this to how it might have been done using UIKit, reiterating the benefits of everything we've done so far.

Questions

1. What does an existing Xcode project see a watchOS project as?
2. What is the entry point for a watchOS app?
3. How can we test our SwiftUI views in watchOS?
4. What framework do we use for sending messages to and from our watchOS app?
5. Why would we use `sendMessage()` over `transferUserInfo()`?

Further reading

- **WatchKit:** https://developer.apple.com/documentation/watchkit
- **App Extensions:** https://developer.apple.com/app-extensions/
- **WatchConnectivity Framework:** https://developer.apple.com/documentation/watchconnectivity
- **UserDefaults:** https://developer.apple.com/documentation/foundation/userdefaults

12
SwiftUI versus UIKit

So far, we've covered many of the benefits of using SwiftUI and also seen how we can utilize UIKit within our SwiftUI projects, but what impact does SwiftUI really have when it comes to developing our apps?

This chapter is intended as a reference and is aimed at those who are new to SwiftUI but have an understanding of UIKit and are looking to make comparisons. It is also intended for those who are brand new to development with SwiftUI and want to learn a little more about the benefits compared to UIKit.

The following topics will be covered in this chapter:

- List view versus UITableView
- Data Binding versus Data Source
- Comparing decoration techniques
- Migrating UIKit so that it's ready for SwiftUI

Technical requirements

For this chapter, you'll need to download Xcode version 11.0 or above from the Apple Mac App Store. You'll also need to be running the latest version of macOS (Catalina or above).

Simply search for Xcode in the App Store and select and download the latest version.

Launch Xcode and follow any additional installation instructions that your system may prompt you for. Once Xcode has fully launched, you'll be ready to go!

List view versus UITableView

Now that we've got a comprehensive understanding of SwiftUI, let's take some time to compare the benefits of SwiftUI against Apple's original UI Framework UIKit. In this section, we'll take a look at the simplicity of a `List()` View in SwiftUI and compare this to how we'd construct a `UITableView()` in UIKit.

Basic UITableView implementation

Let's start by checking out exactly how we'd create a list, similar to the one found in our `ListView.swift` file.

Although we can make use of Storyboards to create `TableViews`, for this comparison, we'll give all our examples programmatically so that we can provide a more direct comparison with the declarative syntax we've just been practicing.

Let's start by creating an instance of a `TableView` in an empty `ViewController`:

```
class ViewController: UIViewController {

    var tableView: UITableView!
    override func viewDidLoad() {

        tableView = UITableView(frame: view.frame)
        view.addSubview(tableView)
    }

}
```

As shown in the highlighted code, we've created the `tableView` variable, which we'll use throughout our class. Next, inside `viewDidLoad()`, we've instantiated our variable and set the size to that of our current view controller. Finally, we've told our view (which sits inside our view controller) that we want to add our `tableView` to it.

Notice how we've had to set up three important things here before we can even get started. The following code shows how we would do this in SwiftUI:

```
struct SwiftUIView: View {
    var body: some View {
        List() { _ in
        }
    }
}
```

Yep, it really is that simple – you'll notice from our previous chapters that the preceding code is missing some things and won't actually compile, but this is a like-for-like reference to what we've just seen in UIKit's TableView(); this would be the SwiftUI equivalent.

Let's go a little deeper and add some content to our UITableView(). We'll start by adding some mock data to our class:

```
var tableView: UITableView!
let mockData = ["Recipe 1", "Recipe 2", "Recipe 3", "Recipe 4", "Recipe 5",
"Recipe 6"]
```

UITableView() uses the delegate pattern, so we need to make sure our ViewController conforms to the UITableView delegate protocol:

```
class ViewController: UIViewController, UITableViewDataSource {
}
```

UITableViewDataSource allows us to overwrite methods that help us construct what data is going to be used and how it will be displayed in our UITableView().

Next, we'll need to tell our tableView that we want to set our current ViewController as the delegate:

```
tableView = UITableView(frame: view.frame)
tableView.dataSource = self
```

Once this is done, by default, Xcode will start to complain and force us to add the required delegate methods (or the least stubs) in order to compile. Now, we need to add the following:

```
func tableView(_ tableView: UITableView, numberOfRowsInSection section:
Int) -> Int
func tableView(_ tableView: UITableView, cellForRowAt indexPath: IndexPath)
-> UITableViewCell
```

numberOfRowsInSection requires you to return an Int that specifies how many rows you intend to show in your list (basically, how many items you have in your mockData).

`cellForRowAt` is where each cell is built up and displayed. `UITableView` will go through each row at a time, setting them up one by one. You can identify each row by inspecting the `IndexPath` that is passed in each time.

Let's add some data to each one:

```
func tableView(_ tableView: UITableView, numberOfRowsInSection section:
Int) -> Int {
    return mockData.count
}
func tableView(_ tableView: UITableView, cellForRowAt indexPath: IndexPath)
-> UITableViewCell {
    let cell = UITableViewCell()
    cell.textLabel?.text = mockData[indexPath.row]
    return cell
}
```

First, we'll return a count of the `mockData` array. This will set up our `UITableView` nicely with the correct amount of rows we intend to use.

Next, we'll return a `UITableViewCell()` with the title of the recipe included. By default, a `UITableViewCell()` has a `UILabel()`, so we can use this to assign text to our cell. To do this on each iteration, we'll need to query our array by using the `indexPath.row` instance that gets passed into `cellForRowAt`.

With that done, we just need to add in more change: we need to invoke the `UITableView` and force it to load our data when our view is rendered. To do this, we will add the following to the end of our `viewDidLoad()` function:

```
tableView = UITableView(frame: view.frame)
tableView.delegate = self
tableView.dataSource = self
view.addSubview(tableView)
tableView.reloadData()
```

With that done, if we launch the app in the simulator, we should see something like this:

Next, we'll look at how to do this in SwiftUI. Since we looked at List Views in the previous chapters, you'll already know how surprisingly easy this is going to be.

Basic SwiftUI List implementation

Now, let's compare how we'd do the exact same thing in SwiftUI:

```
struct SwiftUIView: View {
    let mockData = ["Recipe 1", "Recipe 2", "Recipe 3"]
    var body: some View {
        List(mockData, id: \.self) { recipe in
            Text(recipe)
        }
    }
}
```

That's it, really – excluding the `mockData` variable, we have a total of three lines of code to do the work of everything we covered previously – amazing.

Let's dig a little deeper and have a look at some other comparisons. Remember how, in Chapter 6, *Working with Navigation in SwiftUI*, we looked at how to push to another SwiftUI view by wrapping a simple `NavigationLink` around our List View's iteration?

```
var body: some View {
    List(mockData, id: \.self) { recipe in
        NavigationLink(destination: SecondSwiftUIView()) {
            Text(recipe)
        }
    }
}
```

Again, this is nice and simple. Let's take a look at a comparison in UIKit:

```
func tableView(_ tableView: UITableView, didSelectRowAt indexPath:
IndexPath) {
    present(SecondViewController(), animated: true, completion: nil)
}
```

First, we have to add a new delegate method called `didSelectRowAt`. Again, this delegate is called for each row, which we can identify by referencing the `IndexPath` variable being passed in.

In this section, we made a direct comparison between SwiftUI and UIKit in terms of Lists and UITableViews. Using a similar approach to how we built a List View previously, we saw the clear benefits of how SwiftUI can be used in what should be a very quick and easy implementation.

In the next section, we're going to take a look at how SwiftUI's Data Binding is compared to using a Data Source in UIKit.

Data Binding versus Data Source

Data Sources can play a massive part in building and even (programmatically) designing a `UITableView`. In this section, we'll look at how to best perceive a `UITableViewDataSource` in a way that makes understanding why it works the way it does much clearer.

Then, we'll take a look at a comparison of how we achieve the same thing in SwiftUI.

UIKit – multiple Data Sources

First of all, we must ask the question, why would we want multiple `UITableViewDataSource`? One of the many reasons is simply its reusability.

As we saw in the previous section, we have to conform to the `UITableViewDataSource` delegate and override multiple functions, just in order to get our table to load some data. However, one of the positive sides to all this is the ability to separate out specific code of specific instances.

Referring back to the `IndexPath` we saw being passed into each delegate method, we can easily identify and alter the style or even the type of the `UITableViewCell` being used.

We may, however, decide to reload a whole other set of data and `UITableViewCell` without the need to reload the whole `ViewController`. This is where setting a specific Data Source has its advantages.

The best way to achieve this is by separating the two delegate methods we were forced to conform to earlier into their own classes:

```
class DataSourceA: NSObject, UITableViewDataSource {
    func tableView(_ tableView: UITableView, numberOfRowsInSection section:
Int) -> Int {
        return mockData.count
    }
    func tableView(_ tableView: UITableView, cellForRowAt indexPath:
IndexPath) -> UITableViewCell {
        let cell = UITableViewCell()
        cell.textLabel?.text = mockData[indexPath.row]
```

```
        return cell
    }
}
```

Then, we can simply reference this `datasource` when constructing our `UITableView`, thus giving us various opens when it comes to programmatically assigning multiple Data Sources to one ViewController's `UITableView`:

```
var dataSource: UITableViewDataSource!
override func viewDidLoad() {

    dataSource = DataSourceA()
    tableView.dataSource = dataSource

}
```

Setting the `datasource` in the `UITableView` is as easy as what we saw in the preceding code; however, you must remember to reload the data after you've assigned a new `datasource`, like so:

```
tableView.reloadData()
```

Next, we'll take a look at how we might approach this in SwiftUI by binding our data and using `@ObservedObject` to achieve this.

SwiftUI – handling Data Sources

Following on from where we've just left off with UIKit and UITableViews in SwiftUI, we'll use `@State` in order to invalidate our current layout and force a reload. As a basic implementation, this will work really well and almost do our job for us.

Looking back at our previous example, if we have a mutable variable with our `mockData`, we could simply reassign some data and this would invalidate our layout and reload it with our new data:

```
@State var mockData = ["Recipe 1", "Recipe 2", "Recipe 3"]
```

This would be followed by something like this:

```
mockData = ["Recipe 4", "Recipe 5", "Recipe 6"]
```

This works a treat! Here, we're assigning basic types such as `String`, `Int`, `Bool`, `Array`, and so on. However, our data could be far more complex and won't necessarily be updated from within our View either. That's where `@ObservedObject` comes into play.

Now, if you can think all the way back to `Chapter 3`, *Building Layout and Structure*, you'll remember that we've already covered such a pattern. `PostViewModel()` was an `@ObservableObject`, listening and only publishing changes to our array of `PostModel()` when it received an update from our external API.

As soon as an update was received, our SwiftUI layout was invalidated and our List View was reloaded. Taking this pattern into account when we designed and built our SwiftUI views fulfills the very nature of what SwiftUI does best – unlike UIKit, we don't have to worry about reloading our data at the right time (including making sure we do it at all) and switching over to the correct Data Source – it's all handled gracefully.

In the next section, we'll take a look at the core differences between decorating our views in UIKit and the simplicity of SwiftUI.

Comparing decoration techniques

As many iOS developers will agree, mastering the art of decorating UIViews and manipulating a UIImage can be an art form in itself, to say the least. However, with SwiftUI and the use of modifiers, this pain can be eased quite considerably.

In this section, we'll take a look at and compare modifiers in SwiftUI to see how they hold up against their UIKit counterparts.

Simple decoration made easy

It goes without saying that modifiers in SwiftUI have been a blessing in disguise. Where previously we would have had to make a series of changes in order to make a simple amendment such as a *border with a corner radius*, the use of a one-line modifier does all the hard work for us.

In some cases with UIKit, we could ease the pain a little by creating extensions that we could reuse again and in our current project and across other projects too.

By comparison, you can think of a modifier as an extension of some sort, wrapping up little bundles of complex logic and adding them to one line of code.

Let's start by taking a look at how we can create a border in a `UIButton` with a corner radius:

```
button.backgroundColor = .blue
button.layer.cornerRadius = 15
```

```
button.layer.borderColor = UIColor.black.cgColor
button.layer.borderWidth = 8
button.layer.masksToBounds = true
```

As you can see, there is a lot going on here. After setting the background of the button, we dip into the `CLLayer` to make the adjustment for our border and our corner radius.

Let's take a look at what we would need to do in SwiftUI to achieve this:

```
Text ("New Data")
    .background(Color.blue)
    .overlay(
        RoundedRectangle(cornerRadius: 15)
            .stroke(Color.black, lineWidth: 8)
    )
```

At first glance, you're probably thinking it looks like the same amount of code that we'd use in UIKit, and you wouldn't be wrong. However, if you take a much closer look at the syntax, you'll see it makes a little more sense and is much more developer-friendly.

Again, making use of the declarative syntax, we're telling our `View()` what we want rather than creating it. We're saying we want to add an `Overlay` to our `Text()` view and that the overlay we want is that of a `RoundedRectangle`. The `RoundedRectangle` is just one of many `Overlay` types we can use with the SwiftUI predefining options we may like to use.

Looking a little deeper into the preceding example, you can see that the `RoundedRectangle` itself can accept modifiers in order to further customize the look and feel of the Text View.

Complex decoration made easy

Let's take a look at something a little more complex. Here, we have a gradient effect on a UIKit view – it looks cool and adds a little *something extra* to our control:

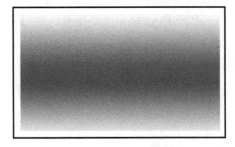

But under the hood and especially to a beginner, this certainly isn't something that's as easy as you might anticipate. Let's take a look at how we would achieve this in UIKit:

```
let gradientView = UIView(frame: view.frame)
let gradientLayer: CAGradientLayer = CAGradientLayer()
gradientLayer.frame.size = gradientView.frame.size
gradientLayer.colors = [UIColor.white.cgColor,
                        UIColor.blue.cgColor,
                        UIColor.green.cgColor]
gradientView.layer.addSublayer(gradientLayer)
view.addSubview(gradientView)
```

We start by creating our UIView. After that, we need to make an instance of a CAGradientLayer() – we set the size, set the array of colors, add the new CAGradientLayer() to the *layer* of our UIView, and then add our UIView to the parent screen view. This isn't a mammoth task, but only when you have the know-how.

Let's do the exact same in SwiftUI:

```
.background(
    LinearGradient(gradient: Gradient(colors: [.white, .blue, .green]),
startPoint: .top, endPoint: .bottom)
    )
```

Starting by making use of the .background modifier, we add a LinearGradient (again, we are telling SwiftUI the style we want to use). This accepts the Gradient() parameter, which we set along with our desired colors and a start and endpoint.

See how the constructors in LinearGradient() and Gradient() are guiding us as to what parameters we expect, thus almost making the whole process self-explanatory.

Another example is a strike through in a UILabel:

```
let attributedString = NSMutableAttributedString(string: "Strike through
me")
attributedString.addAttribute(NSAttributedString.Key.strikethroughStyle,
value: 2, range: NSRange(location: 0, length: attributedString.length))
label.attributedText = attributedString
```

Here, we are making use of NSAttributedString in order to allow us to add the attributed style of strikethrough. First, we need to create an instance of an NSAttributedString from our standard String value. Then, we need to apply the desired attribution to the string by specifying the range of the text that we want to be attributed. Finally, we add this to an attributedText property on our UILabel.

With SwiftUI, we simply do the following:

```
Text("Strike through me")
    .strikethrough()
```

We can add options for an additional option, should we want to:

```
@State var shouldStrike = true
Text("Strike through me")
    .strikethrough(shouldStrike, color: .red)
```

In SwiftUI, we can pass in an *active* flag so that we can `.toggle` the value of a Boolean in order to switch the `strikethrough` off and on.

In the next section, we are going to have a look at how to prepare to migrate existing UIKit controls into our SwiftUI app. We'll do this by familiarizing ourselves with what UIKit has to offer, along with a possible SwiftUI replacement.

Migrating UIKit ready for SwiftUI

So far, we've looked at a direct comparison between UIKit's `TableView()` against SwiftUI's `ListView`, but as common as TableViews are, there are far more options to explore when it comes to migrating to SwiftUI.

Now, due to SwiftUI being new to the scene, not every UIKit control has a SwiftUI equivalent. However, if you ever need to jump back to a particular UIKit control, please refer to the *Using the Representable Protocol* section in Chapter 8, *Networking and Linking to Your Existing App Logic.* We'll cover everything else in this section.

UIStackView

First introduced in iOS 8, `UIStackView` was welcomed with open arms as it allowed for a more flexible layout hierarchy than what was on offer before. UIStackViews allow us to implement vertical and horizontal stacking of independent views without getting bogged down in the complexity of a `UITableView` or a `UICollectionView`:

```
let viewOne = UIView()
let viewTwo = UIView()

let stackView = UIStackView(arrangedSubviews: [viewOne, viewTwo])
stackView.axis = .vertical
stackView.distribution = .fillEqually
```

The preceding snippet of code is how you would programmatically build a `UIStackView`.

> *SwiftUI Equivalent*: *VStack, HStack, and ZStack*

UITextField

Covered in `Chapter 7`, *Creating a Form with States and Data Binding*, `UITextField`, when conforming to the `UITextFieldDelegate` protocol, is a powerful and widely used control in iOS apps.

> *SwiftUI Equivalent*: *TextField and SecureField*

UISwitch

The commonly known *toggle* has been transitioned to the SwiftUI world. Utilizing all the same features, the use of SwiftUI's `@State` binding makes updating logic based on the value of the UISwitches a piece of cake.

> *SwiftUI Equivalent*: *Toggle*

Summary

In this chapter, we looked at the benefits that SwiftUI has to offer over UIKit. Taking `UITableView` as an example, we learned how SwiftUI simplifies the existing delegate pattern given to us by default in UIKit.

Although SwiftUI is beneficial due to its simplicity, UIKit is just as powerful, which is clear from its place in iOS development.

Then, we looked at how using modifiers to decorate our SwiftUI Views compares against UIKit's implementation. With this, we covered border-radius, gradients, and attributed Strings.

In the next chapter, we'll look at how to create basic Animations in SwiftUI and how we can incorporate them into our Recipe app for a bit of added spice (*see what I did there...*)!

Questions

1. What pattern does UIKit use for UITableViews?
2. What protocol does UITableView need to conform to?
3. How does a SwiftUI List look for changes?
4. What modifier do we use in SwiftUI to add a border?

13
Basic Animation in Views

Animations have always played a massive part in any form of development – no matter what language you are coding in. This is no different when developing for iOS applications either. In this chapter, we'll take a look at how we can simply drop animations into our existing app – in some cases, this can be done with just a single line of code.

We'll cover all the various types of animation options available to us, from pulsing buttons to spinning 3D images, and you'll be able to see how the little things we do make such a big difference.

The following topics will be covered in this chapter:

- The fundamental use of Animations
- Exploring animation options
- Rotation and scaling
- Adding Animation to our app

Technical requirements

For this chapter, you'll need to download Xcode version 11.3 or above from the Apple Mac App Store. You'll also need to be running the latest version of macOS (Catalina or above).

Simply search for Xcode in the App Store and select and download the latest version.

Launch Xcode and follow any additional installation instructions that your system may prompt you for. Once Xcode has been fully launched, you'll be ready to go!

The fundamental use of animations

In this section, we are going to learn the basic fundamentals of animation in SwiftUI and start by looking at simple yet effective animations.

We'll start by taking a look at *implicit* animations. With SwiftUI, these don't come much easier. Then, we'll take a look at its counterpart, *explicit* animations, and understand what they have to offer us, both programmatically and over *implicit* animations.

Implicit animations

Let's start by creating a new playground project. Do this by clicking **File** | **New** | **Playground**. Call the project anything you like and add the following code to prepare your playground for SwiftUI:

```
import SwiftUI
import PlaygroundSupport

struct ContentView: View {
    var body: some View {


    }
}

PlaygroundPage.current.setLiveView(ContentView())
```

Now that we've got our playground set up, let's add some content to do. We'll start by adding a basic button and a `Text` view just beneath it:

```
struct ContentView: View {
    var body: some View {
        VStack {
            Button("Tap to Animate") {
            }
            Text("Learn SwiftUI")
        }
    }
}
```

Great! Now, let's make the button disappear and reappear when we click it. We'll achieve this by changing the opacity of the `Text` view (the alpha channel) using `@State` to an `opacity` variable.

Add the following highlighted code. This will allow us to switch the opacity of our Text view:

```
struct ContentView: View {
@State var opacity = 0.0
    var body: some View {
        Button("Tap to Animate") {
            self.opacity = (self.opacity == 1.0) ? 0 : 1.0
        }
        Text("Learn SwiftUI")
            .opacity(opacity)
    }
}
```

Using @State changes, we're modifying the value of the Text view's opacity every time we press the button. A simple ternary operation does a check against the current value of our opacity variable to determine its current state and which value to assign.

Let's take a quick look at this in action by clicking the *run* symbol on the left-hand side of the playground (in the same column as the line numbers), which should be situated on the line next to PlaygroundPage.current.setLiveView(ContentView()):

You'll see that by clicking the button (repeatedly), the text just simply appears and disappears on the screen, just as we would expect. Now, let's add a little magic. Add the following highlighted modifier to the Text view:

```
Text("Learn SwiftUI")
    .opacity(opacity)
    .animation(.default)
```

Yep, that's it – you've added animation to your logic! Albeit small, if you repeatedly click the button, you'll see that the animation is there and much smoother than before.

Notice the .default option we gave to our animation modifier. There are many more options available that we can use in many different ways – don't worry, we'll cover them in a later section, *Exploring animation options*, but let's touch on one quickly now.

Change the animation modifier to the following:

```
.animation(.easeIn(duration: 1))
```

Here, we've added the `easeIn` animation type and set a duration of 1. If you run your playground now, you'll clearly be able to see the animation *ease in* over a duration of time – looks cool, right?

Implicit animations are by far the easiest to add into SwiftUI as all you need to do is add an implicit animation to a View. This means all the aspects of that view will be animated regardless of any visible changes that have been made to their state. Animations will be performed as part of a wider change (such as a higher level binding change).

Next, let's take a look at explicit animations in SwiftUI as a way for us to prepare a specific animation prior to it taking place.

Explicit animations

Our setup is going to be pretty much the same here. Let's create another button with a Text view that we'll use to animate a change:

```
@State var opacity = 0.0
struct ContentView: View {
    var body: some View {
        Button("Tap to Animate") {
            self.opacity = (self.opacity == 1.0) ? 0 : 1.0
        }
        Text("Learn SwiftUI")
            .opacity(opacity)
    }
}
```

This time, we want to *explicitly* tell SwiftUI that the animation is to only occur on an `opacity` change. We do this by adding the following `withAnimation` wrapper to our button action:

```
Button("Tap to Animate") {
    withAnimation {
        self.opacity = (self.opacity == 1.0) ? 0 : 1.0
    }
}
```

Now, SwiftUI knows to only perform the animation on the `opacity` modifier. Let's spruce it up again a little and add our `easeIn` animation to see this in action for ourselves:

```
Button("Tap to Animate") {
    withAnimation(Animation.easeIn(duration: 1)) {
        self.opacity = (self.opacity == 1.0) ? 0 : 1.0
    }
}
```

There we have it – explicit animations in all their glory, with the added benefit of concentrating on the change we need based on the state of a particular view rather than implicitly animating other areas unnecessarily.

In the next section, we'll explore further animation options and learn about the different easing effects available to us in SwiftUI.

Exploring animation options

In the previous section, we learned how to use implicit and explicit animations. By default, we were given a basic animation by SwiftUI, but as we saw with the `easeIn` option, there are many more variants to choose from.

In this section, we'll be covering all the options that are available and how to use them in our implicit and explicit animations.

Easings

The first options we are going to take a look at are easings. Probably one of the most commonly used effects of animation, easings can make even the most basic of animations look polished and finished.

Easings have been around for a while, specifically in web development within **cascading style sheets (CSS)**.

.easeIn

We touched on `easeIn` in the previous section, but for reference, here is how we would use it:

```
Animation.easeIn(duration: 1)
```

The following is a line diagram of ease-in time against value:

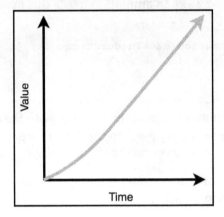

An `easeIn` animation starts off slow and then builds up speed before finalizing the animation effect. Think of a large object falling off an edge and slowly building up momentum as it falls.

.easeOut

You guessed it – the opposite of `easeIn` is `easeOut`:

```
Animation.easeOut(duration: 1)
```

The following is a line diagram of ease-out time against value:

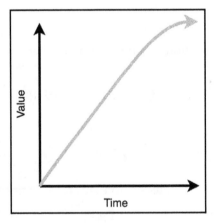

It's often suggested that using `easeOut` should be favored over the use of `easeIn` when performing animations where user attainment or interaction is key. This is due to the slow start that `easeIn` performs, possibly giving a negative impression/impact.

.easeInOut

This is the best of both worlds. It's often used as the default easing option to satisfy both needs and give us the best possible effect:

```
Animation.easeInOut(duration: 1)
```

The following is a line diagram of ease-in-out time against value:

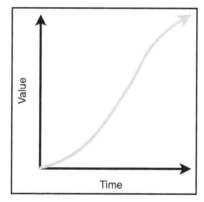

Due to the nature of how `easeInOut` performs, it's advised that you do not perform this animation over a prolonged period of time.

Springs

No matter what anyone says, Spring animations are just plain fun!

Yes, they have their place and in most enterprise apps, and you'd be hard done to find random images and text labels springing around your device screen – but nonetheless, they are still widely used in app development.

Spring and Spring with Damping Fraction were first introduced in iOS 7 as part of the UI overhaul. Although the API has been around since iOS 6, it was only available as a private function that wasn't available to developers.

.spring

First, we have the basic `spring` animation, which can be used in its default state or with damping options:

```
Animation.spring()
Animation.spring(response: 1.0, dampingFraction: 4, blendDuration: 3.0)
```

 Damping Fraction is the amount of drag that's applied to the value being animated as a fraction of an estimate of the amount needed to produce critical damping.

Next, we have `interactiveSpring`, an option that's convenient for `spring` to use with interactive elements (such as a button press):

```
Animation.interactiveSpring()
Animation.interactiveSpring(response: 1.0, dampingFraction: 4,
blendDuration: 3.0)
```

 A convenience is a `spring()` animation with a lower `response` value, intended for driving interactive animations.

Our final Spring option is `interpolatingSpring`:

```
Animation.interpolatingSpring(stiffness: 2, damping: 4)
Animation.interpolatingSpring(mass: 2.0, stiffness: 4.0, damping: 3.0,
initialVelocity: 2.0)
```

 An interpolating spring animation is one that uses a damped spring model to produce values in the range [0, 1] that are then used to interpolate within the [from, to] range of the animated property. It preserves velocity across overlapping animations by adding the effects of each animation.
All of the preceding quotes have been taken from Apple's internal API documentation.

.linear

This is a transition effect that's similar to easings (based on a period of time) but without the initial or final change of inertia:

```
Animation.linear()
Animation.linear(duration: 1)
```

In this section, we looked at the available options we can use when performing an animation in SwiftUI. The majority of the options were around easings and spring animations, although it's not so much about what animation you choose but how you use them. In the next section, we are going to take a look at the rotation and scaling we can perform when using animations. We will learn how to use them in order to manipulate views in SwiftUI.

Rotation and scaling

For those seasoned programmers among us, you'll know that in the past, with a variety of programming languages, manipulating views or screens in terms of rotation, scale, or even geometry required a small understanding of some form of mathematics.

Luckily, with SwifuUI, operations such as rotating and scaling UI elements are a piece of cake. In this section, we're going to look at an API that adds a 3D feel to an element being rotated.

Rotation

Let's start by looking at rotation. We'll begin by creating another button. This time, we'll decorate it a little (you'll see why later):

```
struct ContentView: View {
    var body: some View {

        Button("Rotate") {
        }
        .padding(10)
        .background(Color.green)
        .foregroundColor(.white)
        .clipShape(Circle())
    }

}
```

This will give us a nice and simple circular button. Now, we're going to add the following modifier:

```
.rotationEffect(Angle(degrees: 360))
```

The rotation effect modifier will do exactly as it says – it requires you to pass in an `Angle()` with either the option to use degrees or radians for the desire rotation amount.

Next, let's create a `@State` variable that will hold the value of our degrees:

```
@State var rotation = 1440.0
```

We'll give this the default value of `1440.0` (basically 360 * 4) so that we get a couple of good rotations on our view.

Next, let's create an explicit animation and change the state of this variable when our button is clicked:

```
Button("Rotate") {
    withAnimation {
        self.rotation = self.rotation == 1440 ? 0 : 1440
    }
}
```

Again, we are using a ternary operator to check the current value and reset it if applicable (so we can keep clicking to repeat the animation).

Now, it's time to add in our rotation modifier:

```
Button("Rotate") {
    withAnimation {
        self.rotation = self.rotation == 1440 ? 0 : 1440
    }
}
.padding(10)
.background(Color.green)
.foregroundColor(.white)
.clipShape(Circle())
.rotationEffect(Angle(degrees: rotation))
```

Using the same principles that we used previously, we can now explicitly animate the change in the `Angle` of our view, which in turn will cause the `rotationEffect` modifier to perform its magic – go on, give it a go!

3D rotation

Working almost identically to `.rotationEffect`, the 3D rotation effect is another modifier that will attempt to add a 3D mask to the view you are trying to rotate, thus giving it an almost *embossed* effect when it spins:

```
.rotation3DEffect(.degrees(360), axis: (x: 0, y: 1, z: 0))
```

One noticeable difference with `rotation3DEffect` is that it requires an axis to base the rotation off.

From the preceding code snippet, setting the *y* axis allows our view to spin from left to right or vice versa on a vertical point (like a signpost would do in a cartoon!).

The *x* axis will rotate from top to bottom and the *z* axis will spin the view *around*, much like `rotationEffect` did.

Scaling

Scaling is another type of element manipulation that previously would have required some calculations that may have eluded some of us.

However, using the same methods as we did with the opacity animation, along with the use of a simple modifier, we can quickly and efficiently scale elements however we want.

Let's have a go by creating another button, just like we did earlier:

```
Button("Scale") {
    withAnimation {
        // Add scale logic here...
    }
}
.padding(10)
.background(Color.green)
.foregroundColor(.white)
.clipShape(Circle())
```

Now, let's take a look at our scale modifier:

```
.scaleEffect(1)
```

Yep, it's really that easy! Actually, the only real difference here is the logic that's used to calculate the increase and decrease of the scale effect. Let's add that now.

First, we'll create our `@State` variable:

```
@State var scaleEffect: CGFloat = 1
```

Now, let's add in the logic to increase and decrease this with every button click:

```
Button("Scale") {
    withAnimation {
        if abs(self.scaleEffect-1.0) < 0.01 {
            self.scaleEffect += 0.4
        } else {
            self.scaleEffect -= 0.4
        }
    }
}
```

Now, before we carry on, let's take a look at the start of our condition:

```
abs(self.scaleEffect-1.0) < 0.01
```

I know what you're thinking – what is this all about? It's not too important right now as we're only using this as an example to move back and forth in our animation, but in a nutshell, the preceding code is the equivalent to `self.scaleEffect == 1`, but as we are dealing with floating points, we have to perform this small calculation. For more information on floating-point calculations, take a look at the link provided in the *Further reading* section.

Finally, let's add the modifier for our button:

```
.padding(10)
.background(Color.green)
.foregroundColor(.white)
.clipShape(Circle())
.scaleEffect(scaleEffect)
```

With that done, it's time to try it out. With each click of the button, you should see the button scale up and down. Try it with one of the `Spring()` animations to give your button a bit more character – go on, have a play and experiment with all the animation options available!

In the next section, we're going to take what we have learned so far in this chapter and apply that to our app.

Adding animation to our app

In the previous sections, we learned a lot about animations in SwiftUI and with the helping hand of Swift Playground, we've been able to demonstrate and see these in action. But there's nothing like practicing them in the real world! In this section, we'll add some of the tricks we've learned throughout this chapter directly into our app. Even with the smallest of changes, you'll instantly be able to see the impact animations have.

Spinning star

Now, let's head on over to our Recipe app and make some changes ourselves. We'll start by heading on over to `RecipeDetailView.swift` and finding our favorite button. Add the following highlighted code to add a little *spin* to our selection:

```
Button(action: {
    Helper.addRemoveFavourite(recipe: self.recipe)
    self.recipe.favourite.toggle()
    withAnimation(.spring()) {
        self.angle = self.angle == 1080 ? 0 : 1080
    }
}) {
    Image(systemName: isFavourite ? "star.fill" : "star")
        .resizable()
        .aspectRatio(contentMode: .fit)
}
.rotationEffect(.degrees(angle))
.frame(height: 45)
```

Here, we've added an explicit animation to our star view. Looking at the *action* in our button, it's clear we're performing a `.spring()` animation when we set the angle of our rotation effect.

Then, we added the `rotationEffect` modifier and set the degrees to the value of our angle variable, which we'll need to set as follows:

```
@State private var angle: Double = 0
```

Go ahead – compile and run the project and check it out. You'll see the immediate impact of such a small animation.

Find all the other places in the app that have the favorites star and apply this animation there too.

Fading image

Still in `RecipeDetailView.swift`, let's make a change to our main image. By design, the image should just appear on the screen when the view is loaded, but with a small and very subtle animation, we can give it a much more grand entrance.

Add the following highlighted changes to the Image view, at the top of our view:

```
Image(uiImage: recipe.image)
    .resizable()
    .aspectRatio(contentMode: .fill)
    .frame(maxWidth: 400, maxHeight: 200)
    .clipShape(RoundedRectangle(cornerRadius: 10))
    .opacity(imageOpacity)
    .onAppear {
        withAnimation(Animation.easeIn(duration: 2.6).delay(0.4)) {
            self.imageOpacity = 1
        }
    }
```

We'll start by adding the `.opacity` modifier to our Image view and setting this with the value from the `imageOpacity` variable:

```
@State private var imageOpacity = 0.0
```

Next, we'll need to do something we've not yet covered. Since we are not invoking the animation via a button click and are looking to do this when our view firsts loads, we'll set our explicit animation to occur within a `.onAppear` modifier.

Also, notice how we've tweaked some of the animation values in order to get the desired effect. We've set `.easeIn` to `2.4` and also added a `.delay` of `0.4` to our animation in order to allow time for our view to load before performing the actual animation.

Rotating the 3D action button

Finally, let's take a look at how well the `rotation3DEffect` works. Head on over to `AddRecipeView.swift` and find the `Button` and Image view that we use to choose an image from our library.

Make the following highlighted changes:

```
Button(action: {
    DispatchQueue.main.asyncAfter(deadline: .now() + 0.4) {
        self.showingImagePicker.toggle()
```

```
    }
    self.angle = self.angle == 360 ? 0 : 360
}) {
Image(uiImage: self.libraryImage ?? (UIImage(named: "placeholder-add-
image") ?? UIImage()))
    .resizable()
    .aspectRatio(contentMode: .fit)
    .clipShape(Circle())
    .overlay(Circle().stroke(Color.purple, lineWidth: 3).shadow(radius:
10))
    .frame(maxWidth: .infinity, maxHeight: 230)
    .padding(6)
}
.rotation3DEffect(.degrees(angle), axis: (x: 0, y: 1, z: 0))
.animation(.spring())
```

In this example, we're going to add an implicit animation so that when we update an `angle`
variable by clicking our button, our image will spin.

Add the following `@State` variable outside of our body view:

```
@State private var angle: Double = 0
```

Now, add the following logic to our button's action:

```
self.angle = self.angle == 360 ? 0 : 360
```

Notice again how we use our ternary operator in order to allow rotation to occur on each
click (without the need for resetting the value).

Finally, we'll add our required modifiers:

```
.rotation3DEffect(.degrees(angle), axis: (x: 0, y: 1, z: 0))
.animation(.spring())
```

Go ahead and run the app – how does it look? Truthfully, it looks good until the `.sheet` is
presented and takes away all its glory. Due to this, we need to make a minor change to
delay the `.sheet` presenting so that we can see the animation in full.

Make the following highlighted change inside the button's action:

```
Button(action: {
    DispatchQueue.main.asyncAfter(deadline: .now() + 0.4) {
        self.showingImagePicker.toggle()
    }
    self.angle = self.angle == 360 ? 0 : 360
}) {
```

This method isn't new to SwiftUI. It uses something called **Grand Central Dispatch (GCD)**, which has been around since the Objective-C days in both iOS and Mac development. In this instance, it's a way of asynchronously delaying the login enclosed within its closure.

Inside the GCD closure, we'll add our existing logic to toggle our `showingImagePicker` Boolean, thus, in turn, delaying when our `.sheet` is presented.

With this change made, go ahead and rerun the app and check out the 3D effect in all its glory. You'll see that, along with our border and the image we've chosen, SwiftUI does a real good job of embossing our images when it spins – looks pretty cool, right?

Summary

In this chapter, we've touched on the core basics of animation in SwiftUI. We've learned about the differences between explicit and implicit animations and when best to use one or the other. We've referenced all the various animation options available to use, from the various types of *easings* to all the options that *springs* have to offer.

Next, we looked at scaling and rotation and put both into practice with the animation types that we just covered, thereby allowing us to experiment with various settings to get our desired effect.

Finally, we took everything we learned from the previous sections and added this to our existing Recipe app. We finished this off by showing you how well the `.rotation3DEffect` animation works.

In the next chapter, we're going to be continuing with the theme of animations and take a look at how transitions work in SwiftUI, as well as how we can incorporate these into our Recipe app.

Questions

1. Name the two ways of performing animations in SwiftUI.
2. Name three of the animation types we have available.
3. What rotation options are available to us?
4. What modifier would we use if we needed to animate without user invocation?
5. How would we achieve postponing an animation for a set period of time?

Further reading

- **Dispatch:** `https://developer.apple.com/documentation/DISPATCH`
- **Floating Points:** `https://floating-point-gui.de/`

14
Animations in Transitions

As we saw in `Chapter 13`, *Basic Animation in Views*, animations can play a part in making a big difference to any app, no matter how small the change is. But if there is one thing that can complement an animation, it's a transition effect.

In this chapter, we are going to start by covering the basic transitions available to us from SwiftUI. We'll look at how and when we can use these with animations and what effect they'll have on our views.

We'll also cover some slightly more advanced syntax in order to not only optimize our code but improve how the animation takes place.

Once we've done that, we'll go back to our Recipe app for the last time and add some finishing touches.

The following topics will be covered in this chapter:

- Basic transitions
- Advanced transitions
- Adding transitions to our app

Technical requirements

For this chapter, you'll need to download Xcode version 11.3 or above from the Apple Mac App Store. You'll also need to be running the latest version of macOS (Catalina or above).

Simply search for `Xcode` in the AppStore and select and download the latest version.

Launch Xcode and follow any additional installation instructions that your system may prompt you for. Once Xcode has fully launched, you'll be ready to go.

Basic transitions

Let's start by taking a look at how the simplest of transitions can make a big difference in SwiftUI. In this section, we'll cover when and how to use the transition modifier along with the various options available to us.

Invoking a basic transition

We'll again create a SwiftUI playground in order to test some of these examples out (see Chapter 13, *Basic Animation in Views*, on how we created a playground for use in SwiftUI).

We'll start by creating a simple button with a text view that will sit just beneath it:

```
VStack {
    Button("Basic Transitions") {
        // Add logic here...
    }
    Text("Learn SwiftUI")
}
```

Nice and simple to start with, but our main intention here is to use transitions to bring in our text view when the button is clicked. Let's start by adding a @State variable and some conditional logic to make this happen:

```
@State var transition = false
```

Then we'll add the following highlighted changes:

```
Button("Basic Transitions") {
    self.transition.toggle()
}
if transition {
    Text("Learn SwiftUI")
}
```

Go ahead and run the code in the playground's canvas. Just as we expected, you should see the text view appear when you click the button.

Now for the... not so complex part: we'll add a simple modifier to our text view and wrap our self.transitions.toggle() in an animation block:

```
Button("Basic Transitions") {
    withAnimation {
        self.transition.toggle()
    }
```

```
    }
if transition {
    Text("Learn SwiftUI")
        .transition(.slide)
    }
```

Go ahead and run the playground and test it out for yourself—all going well, you should see the text view slide into a transition nicely.

 Apple has recently made a change so that transitions can only be used alongside *Explicit* animations.

With that done, you'll have noticed that we passed in the `.slide` enum to our transition modifier. Let's take a look at the other options available to us.

Transition modifier options

There are various options available to us within the basic transition modifier. Let's start by taking a look at them one at a time. I've included direct quotes from the Apple API documentation too (where available):

- `.opacity`:

    A transition from transparent to opaque on insertion and opaque to transparent on removal

    `.transition(.opacity)`

- `.scale`:

    No overview available (but basically transitions the view into another view by scaling to size)

    `.transition(.scale)`

- `.identity`:

    A transition that returns the input view, unmodified, as the output view

    `.transition(.identity)`

- `.slide:`

  A transition that inserts by moving in from the leading edge, and removes by moving out toward the trailing edge

  `.transition(.slide)`

The preceding options are more than enough to get you started, but let's take a look at some other ways that we can transition views around.

Moving views with transitions

Another transition option we have is `.move`:

```
.transition(.move(edge: .top))
```

With this option and its accompanying animation, we can transition the view to the chosen *edge* of a view (`.top`, `.leading`, `.bottom`, `.trailing`).

Add this into your previous playground code and have a go; change the enum values to see all the options.

As we mentioned, the transition will only work as long as it is accompanied by an animation (in our case, an explicit animation). As we're not specifying an animation type, SwiftUI will automatically use the `.default` animation provided by the framework.

Let's take what we've learned from Chapter 13, *Basic Animation in Views*, and spruce up both our animation and transition in one go:

```
Button("Basic Transitions") {
    withAnimation(.interpolatingSpring(stiffness: 40.0, damping: 1.0)) {
        self.transition.toggle()
    }
}
.padding(.top, 15)
if transition {
    Text("Learn SwiftUI")
        .transition(.move(edge: .bottom))
}
```

With this change, you'll see the Text view bounce into life from the bottom of its frame, springing up and down until it finally finds its place.

It's nice how we can see both sides of animations and transitions start to come together, but with some intelligent syntax, we can make them work together even more efficiently.

In the next section, we'll take a look at some more advanced transition options, specifically looking at asymmetric transitions and how we can combine them with inline animations.

Advanced transitions

As we saw in the previous section, combining both animations and transitions needn't be a headache. Yet, in addition to the basic approach, SwiftUI also gives us some alternative options to work with, allowing for more creativity in how we handle not only transitions on their own, but also alongside our existing animation options.

Asymmetric transitions

Asymmetric transitions are a way of adding and removing views based on their current state without the need for additional or duplicated logic.

Let's take a look at our previous example and see how we would achieve this:

```
Button("Basic Transitions") {
    withAnimation {
        self.transition.toggle()
    }
}
if transition {
    Text("Learn SwiftUI (click me again)")
        .transition(.asymmetric(insertion: .opacity, removal: .scale))
}
```

The highlighted code in the preceding snippet is all we need to do. Our `.transition` modifier accepts a type of `.asymmetric`, which in turn asks for both `insertion` and `removal` parameters:

- `insertion` will be the initial transition performed when our `if` statement is satisfied.
- `removal` will occur when the state is reversed; in our example, this causes the view to transition away using a `.scale`.

As previously mentioned, these transitions are only possible with their accompanying animation, which leaves the window wide open for further animation types to be added into the mix.

Combined transitions

This is where it starts to get interesting. Using a combined transition allows you to perform two transitions simultaneously. Let's take a look at how we would construct this modifier:

```
.transition(AnyTransition.opacity.combined(with: .slide))
```

Here, we start by selecting the first transition in question, `AnyTransition.opacity`. Then, we use the combined function to add a `.slide` effect to the mix.

Try it out—see how seamlessly it works? Remember that you'll still need an accompanying animation to go with it, but more on how we can help tackle that in a moment.

Using asymmetric, combined, and inline animations together

Now that we've covered a couple of the more advanced options with transitions, let's take a look at how we can make them all work seamlessly together.

We'll start by merging both **asymmetric** and **combined** transitions together:

```
.transition(.asymmetric(insertion: AnyTransition.opacity.combined(with:
.slide), removal: .scale))
```

As you can see from the preceding code, we've added the combined function within our `insertion` parameter—go ahead and try it for yourself!

Another thing that you've heard me mention quite a few times in this chapter is the following:

> *Remember that you'll still need an accompanying animation.*

Well, that's not always the case. Let's take a look at how we can adjust our code to include the explicit animation so that we don't have to worry about it:

```
Button("Basic Transitions") {
    self.transition.toggle()
}
.padding(.top, 15)
if transition {
    Text("Learn SwiftUI (click me again)")
        .transition(AnyTransition.opacity.combined(with:
.slide).animation(.easeInOut(duration: 1.0)))
}
```

With this approach, we can forget about our `withAnimation` wrapper and bring the whole transition inline.

We can even go a step further and combine all three together:

```
.transition(.asymmetric(insertion: AnyTransition.opacity.combined(with:
.slide).animation(.easeInOut(duration: 1.0)), removal: .opacity)
```

I know that that's not everyone's cup of tea, but the options are there and work just as efficiently as they would any other way.

In the next section, we'll learn how to put everything we've done in the previous sections into practice by adding transitions straight into our recipe app.

Adding transitions to our app

Now that we've mastered the art of basic transitions, let's continue to work these into our app so we can really fine-tune our UI.

In this section, we'll add some basic transitions to our app, looking specifically at moving text with transitions. Then we'll take what we have learned with advanced transitions by incorporating asymmetric and combined transitions alongside the existing animations that we added in `Chapter 13`, *Basic Animation in Views*.

Transition validation

We'll start off with something simple. Head on over to `AddRecipeView.swift` and add the following `@State` variable:

```
@State private var validated = false
```

Now add the following just below your **Save** button:

```
if validated {
    Text("* Please give your recipe a name")
        .foregroundColor(.red)
        .bold()
        .transition(.move(edge: .top))
}
```

Here, we'll perform a `.transition(.move(edge: .top))` when our validated variable is switched, so let's add the logic for that now in our **Save** button. Make the following highlighted changes:

```
Button(action: {
    if self.recipeName != "" {
        self.saveRecipe()
        self.presentationMode.wrappedValue.dismiss()
    } else {
        withAnimation {
            self.validated.toggle()
        }
    }
}) {
    Text("Save")
}
```

Then we check to see if the `recipeName` has a value. If it does, then we continue to our `saveRecipe()` function as normal; if not, we fall back on our `else` statement and perform an animation on our validated variable, which in turn will cause the recently added `if` statement to be satisfied and our validation message to transition in:

Save

* Please give your recipe a name

It's as simple as that. Next, we're going to look at some of the existing animations that we added and see how we implement the best of both animations and transitions.

Asymmetric transition – loading state

In this section, we are going to transition a text view, which lets the user know when they are requesting a remote image from our external API. Once the loading is complete and our image is displayed, we'll then transition out the text view.

Staying within `AddRecipeView.swift`, add the following `@State` variable into our struct:

```
@State var loadingImage = false
```

Next, add the following code just underneath the recipe image view:

```
if loadingImage {
    Text("Fetching Random Image")
        .transition(.asymmetric(insertion: .opacity, removal: .scale))
}
```

Here, we've wrapped our Text view around a condition based on the current Boolean value of our `loadingImage` variable. Now let's add in the animation and set the state of the variable when we request an image.

Make the following highlighted change:

```
Button(action: {
    self.getRandomImage()
    withAnimation {
        self.loadingImage.toggle()
    }
}) {
    Text("Random Image")
}
```

Now we just need to transition out the message once the image has loaded. Make the following highlighted changes in our `getRandomImage()` function:

```
NetworkHelper.loadData(url: url) { (image) in
    self.libraryImage = image
    self.loadingImage.toggle()
}
```

With all that done, fire up the simulator and let's see it in action. All going well, you should see something like this:

Transitions and animations can be used for a plethora of things, but sometimes it's easy to get carried away. The saying 'less is more' is very true in this scenario, especially as we've seen that such a small change can have such a big impact.

Summary

In this chapter, we started by taking a look at basic transitions and how we can invoke them using animations we learned about in Chapter 13, *Basic Animations in Views*. We then covered the range of modifiers available to us, including scaling, opacity, and sliding.

From this, we took a deep dive into the more advanced options and saw how asymmetric transitions work by giving us entry and exit points for a specific transition. We then looked at how to combine transitions, which allowed us to use the power of two different transitions in one go.

Finally, we took everything we learned from our advanced transitions and brought them together harmoniously to really show off the power of animations and transitions in SwiftUI.

In the next chapter, we'll take a look at how to tackle testing and debugging, and how we as the developer can make Xcode work for us.

Questions

1. What type of animation is required for a transition to work?
2. Name three of the transition options available to us.
3. How would we adjust a view with a transition?
4. What is the difference between asymmetric and combined transitions?

15
Testing in SwiftUI

In this chapter, we'll explore the fundamentals of testing and debugging and see how we can use the excellent tools already built into Xcode to achieve this.

We'll learn how to incorporate XCTest into our Recipe app for both UI and Unit Test and then go on to write our very own test that we can run against our project.

Finally, we'll cover debugging and how we can stop the process of our app in real-time and use certain tools and commands to inspect elements right within Xcode.

The following topics will be covered in this chapter:

- Creating our first UI test project and tests
- Creating our first Unit Test project and tests
- Debugging in SwiftUI

Technical requirements

For this chapter, you'll need to download Xcode version 11.3 or above from the Apple Mac App Store. You'll also need to be running the latest version of macOS (Catalina or above).

Simply search for Xcode in the App Store and select and download the latest version.

Launch Xcode and follow any additional installation instructions that your system may prompt you for. Once Xcode has been fully launched, you'll be ready to go!

Creating a UI/Unit Test project

Testing plays a massive part in any form of software development, from a human being sitting at a desk and running through a script of what to test and what results are expected, to automated tests running hourly or every time a change is made to a particular code base.

Regardless of how small or big your app is, one way or another, testing should always play a fundamental part in your app's development process.

In this section, we are going to take a look at two ways we can integrate tests in our app from a developer's perspective: by using tools that are built into Xcode and a process that can seamlessly be added into our project.

Creating a UI test project

We'll start by taking a look at UI Tests – or automation tests, as they are sometimes known (although most variations of developer tests are automated).

UI tests allow us to validate certain aspects of our apps from a visual perspective of the user's *happy path* of what is expected from the app. Let's start by adding a UITest project to our existing Recipe app.

In our existing project, click **File** | **New** | **Target**. Once the menu is open, make sure the iOS tab is selected and search for Test in the search box. Then, highlight UI Testing Bundle and click Next:

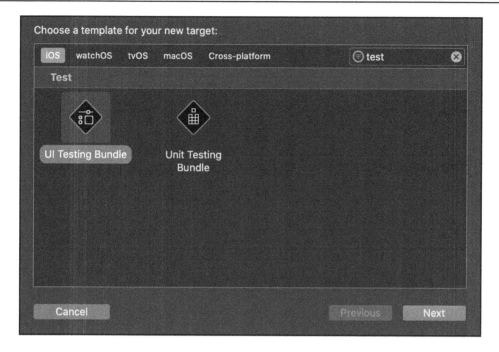

Click **Next** and then using the preselected defaults. On the next screen, click **Create**.

Now, if you take a look inside Xcode, you'll see that a new target has been created:

In addition, a new set of files to accompany the new target will have also been created:

With all that done, let's take a look at the `UITest` file that has been generated for us. Highlight the `My_Favourite_RecipesUITests.swift` file to do so.

As usual, Xcode has generated some nice boilerplate templates for us. All of this can be useful when writing complex and in-depth UI Tests, but for the scope of this book, we can strip back a good portion of it.

Remove all the functions and code comments from inside the test class, apart from the following two:

```
override func setUp() {
}

func testExample() {
}
```

We'll look at the `setUp()` function a bit later, but as you can see, this is an overridden function that will be called whenever your suite or individual tests are run.

Next is `testExample()`. This is our very first UI Test (well done!). However, as you can see, it's as useful as a chocolate fireguard... Let's change that by creating our very first UI Test.

Writing our very first UI Test

Let's start by looking at naming conventions for UI Tests. The key (and best practice) to UI Tests – or any test functions, for that matter – is a good name. Try and write the function name as if you were describing the action you are taking, along with the expected result.

Rename the `testExample()` function to `testCanTapMapButton()`. The key here is to always start your function names with the word `test`. This is how Xcode and XCTest are able to identify your tests.

As you've probably gathered by the description, our first UI Test is going to check that not only is the map button visible, but if it is tappable too, since this is what we expect from the app when it's launched.

Make the following highlighted amendment to the function:

```
func testCanTapMapButton() {
    let app = XCUIApplication()
    app.launch()
    app.buttons["accessibility.map.button"].tap()
}
```

Let's go through this one line at a time. First, we create an instance of `XCUIApplication()`. This instance is a reference to the app in our main project and it's from here where we will invoke all our UI Test requests.

Next, we launch the app, which, as you'll see shortly, will be done in the simulator, just as it would when debugging.

Now, we're getting to the interesting part. Here, you can see that we are referencing `app.buttons`, which is a list of all the button elements on our screen at that time. We select a button that has an identifier of `accessibility.map.button` and performs a `.tap()`.

In layman's terms, we find a specific button and tap on it (just like a user would). If `XCTest` is able to do this, our test will pass, but if it doesn't for some reason, it won't.

Let's run the test to see how we do. We can do this one of two ways. The first is by pressing *command + U* on the keyboard or secondly by clicking on the little diamond next to our function name, as shown here:

So, did your test pass or fail? I'm guessing that your test should have failed and that you were presented with the red diamond of shame and the following error message from Xcode: `Failed to get matching snapshot: No matches found for Elements matching predicate "accessibility.map.button"`:

Don't worry – this is a simple fix. The actual problem is exactly what the error message is saying: `XCTest` is unable to find a button with the identifier of `accessibility.map.button`. Why, you ask? Because we haven't given our button this identifier yet.

Head on over to `ContentView.swift` and add the following highlighted modifier to our navigation map button:

```
}.sheet(isPresented: $showMap) {
    RecipeMapView(filter: self.$filter)
}
.accessibility(identifier: "accessibility.map.button")
```

In order to identify elements, `XCTest` harnesses the power of Accessibility tags in order for us to perform our tests.

One thing I'm a firm believer of is that Accessibility and UI Testing can work in harmony together as they make your app accessible and, in turn, make it easier to write UI Tests, thus forcing a good portion of accessibility into your app.

If you are interested in learning more about mobile accessibility, my good friend Rob Whitaker (@RobRWAPP) runs and maintains a fantastic blog over at https://mobilea11y.com/ on the subject.

Go ahead and run your test again – what do you see?

Your test has passed! Seeing that green diamond is a thing of beauty! Now, let's crack on and write some more tests.

Writing multiple UI Tests

Now, let's add some more UI Tests regarding the navigation buttons. Here are some more I've created. Copy these into your project and see if you can add the relevant accessibility modifiers to get them to pass. Go on – I know you can do it!

```
func testCanTapFilterButton() {
    let app = XCUIApplication()
    app.launch()
    app.buttons["accessibility.filter.button"].tap()
}
func testCanTapAddButton() {
    let app = XCUIApplication()
    app.launch()
    app.buttons["accessibility.add.button"].tap()
}
```

Did they pass? I'm sure they did, but if you are struggling, just take a look at the sample project for this chapter and it will point you in the right direction.

Now, let's take a closer look at all three UI Tests we have. Notice anything? There's a lot of duplication, especially in terms of creating our XCUIApplication() instance and launching it. This is where our setUp() method comes in handy.

Make the following highlighted changes to your test class:

```
let app = XCUIApplication()
    override func setUp() {
        app.launch()
    }
```

Here, we are creating an instance of our `XCUIApplication` outside of our functions and performing a `.launch()` when our suite of tests starts. With that done, you should be able to trim down your tests, as shown here:

```
func testCanTapMapButton() {
    app.buttons["accessibility.map.button"].tap()
}
func testCanTapFilterButton() {
    app.buttons["accessibility.filter.button"].tap()
}
func testCanTapAddButton() {
    app.buttons["accessibility.add.button"].tap()
}
```

That's much better! With this in mind, you have to remember that each test now shares the same launch instance of your application. Should you want to launch your test from a fresh instance of your app for any reason, simply revert that function to use a local version of `XCUIApplicaton()`.

Nesting UI Tests

Another trick we can perform is making use of existing tests we've already written in order to help aid new tests, such as if we want to check something on our `AddRecipeDetail` view. But first, we need to get there.

 In the world of Unit Tests (covered in the next section), tests like these are commonly referred to as integration tests. This is because they are testing the integration between pieces of logic by testing one function's dependency on another.

Add the following new test to your test class:

```
func testCanAddRecipeImage() {
    testCanTapAddButton()
    app.buttons["accessibility.add.image.button"].tap()
}
```

As you can see, we are simply calling an existing test, `testCanTapAddButton()`, to get to the `AddRecipeView` view. From there, we can continue with our desired test, which in this case checks whether we can tap on the **Add Image** button.

Testing with assertions

We're well on our way now with writing our UI Tests, so let's take a look at assertions. Assertions allow us to test the outcome of a particular scenario; for example, if a value (such as a String) should equal (or not equal) another value or whether an Integer should be equal to, greater than, or less than a particular value.

Let's make a new UI Test based around our `AddRecipeView`:

```
func testAddIngredientsAddsToList() {
    testCanTapAddButton()
    let textField = app.textFields["accessibility.ingredient.textfield"]
    textField.tap()
    textField.typeText("Milk")
    app.buttons["accessibility.ingredient.add.button"].tap()
    XCTAssertTrue(app.staticTexts["accessibility.ingredient.list"].exists)
}
```

Again, we've called upon another existing function to get where we want to be. Here, we've identified a specific `TextField` and tapped on this to bring it into focus (just like a user would to bring up the keyboard). Then, we've used `.typeText("")` to enter a test so that we can `.tap()` the Add button.

Finally, we can now perform our assertion. Looking at our logic in `AddRecipeView.swift`, we only create the list if something has been added to it, so for our assertion, we're looking for the `staticTexts` identifier in question and checking if it `.exists`.

With our `XCTestAssertTrue` wrapped around this logic, `XCTest` will either pass or fail the test based on the outcome. Try it for yourself – don't forget to add the `accessibilityIdentifier` modifiers in the required places.

In this section, we learned all about UI Tests and how to set up a specific target just for the tests within our existing Xcode project. Then, we looked at the structure of running each test and created multiple UI Tests, some of which can be integrated with each other, in order to test the required user journey.

In the next section, we'll create our first Unit Test and learn about the differences between them and UI Tests.

Creating our first Unit Test project and tests

In this section, we are going to take a look at the other side of the testing pond and discover what Unit Tests are and why they are just as important as UI Tests. We'll start by creating a Unit Test project within our current Xcode project and create our first test.

Creating a Unit Test project

As opposed to UI Tests, Unit Tests are designed to test specific pieces of logic within your app. For example, you may have a function that calculates a complex algorithm, which would then be used in multiple places within your app.

Writing a Unit Test for this function will give you the confidence of being able to update your logic without having to worry about any breaking changes.

In our existing project, click **File** | **New** | **Target**. Once the menu is open, make sure the **iOS** tab is selected and search for Test in the search box. Then, highlight **Unit Testing Bundle** and click **Next**:

Click **Next**. Use the defaults that have been preselected on the next screen and click **Create**.

Now, if you take a look inside Xcode, you'll see a new target has been created, just like when we created our UI Test target:

Again, a new set of files to accompany the new target has also been created:

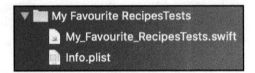

Now, let's take a look at the Unit Test file that has been generated for us. Highlight the `My_Favourite_RecipesTests.swift` file to do so.

Once again, Xcode has generated some nice boilerplate templates for us. Let's strip some of this back again so that we're left with the following functions:

```
override func setUp() {
}

func testExample() {
}
```

Look familiar? Yep, thought so... `XCTest` works very similarly across the board with both Unit Test and UI Tests, so the basic implementation is the same.

Writing our very first Unit Test

Now that we're set up, let's get straight into it and start writing our first Unit Test. Copy the following into your test class (you can remove `testExample()`):

```
func testIfGetCountriesHasItems() {
    XCTAssertTrue(Helper.getCountries().count > 0)
}
```

We'll start with something nice and simple. Inside our `Helper` method, we have a function called `getCounties()` that we'll always need to return an array of countries for our app to work. So, with the use of `XCAssertTrue`, we can write a very quick one-liner Unit Test that checks if our helper function actually returns some results.

We can also write this like so:

```
XCTAssertGreaterThan(Helper.getCountries().count, 0)
```

Using the `XCTAssertGreaterThan` assertion allows us to explicitly set a minimum value that must be met.

Let's look at what else we can test in our app. Here is another example of a valid Unit Test we could run:

```
func testThatGetCoordinatesReturnsCorrectLatLon() {
    let locationOne = Helper.getCoordinates(country: "Spain")
    XCTAssertEqual(locationOne.latitude, 41.383)
    XCTAssertEqual(locationOne.longitude, 2.183)
    let locationTwo = Helper.getCoordinates(country: "UK")
    XCTAssertEqual(locationTwo.latitude, 53.483959)
    XCTAssertEqual(locationTwo.longitude, -2.244644)
}
```

Here, we are checking against our `getCoordinates()` helper by asserting the result of the function with the set data we are passing in. So, in our case, if anyone messes with the coordinates for `"Spain"`, our Unit Test will fail. This might be okay since the change could indeed be intentional, but at least we are aware of it and are able to adjust our test case accordingly.

Unit Testing conclusion

The main focus of this book is UI and we've not had to write a great deal of hard logic or algorithms, so I just wanted to touch on Unit Testing so that you can consider it when you write your first app.

The key to successful Unit Testing is finding a way to implement it that suits you. There are many different approaches, such as **test-driven development** (**TDD**), which is where a developer would write the Unit Test first (which, in turn, would fail) and then write the function accordingly in order to make the test pass. Once the test passes, you could then refactor your code with the safe knowledge that any breaking changes would be picked up by your Unit Test.

Unit Tests can be really powerful, but you must remember that the true nature of Unit Testing is to test one function. If the function you are testing requires data from another source (or function), then this data must be mocked up and injected into your test. The use of changing functions together to perform tests is called integration tests.

In the next section, we are going to take a look at debugging and the options available to us in Xcode that can help make our life a little easier when we run into any problems.

Debugging in SwiftUI

In the olden days, the thought of your IDE being able to debug your application was unheard of – you could spend hours looking for that bug only to find it was a missing semicolon.

In this section, we'll cover the options available to us in Xcode that will help make our daily lives just a little easier. We'll start by taking a look at how to add breakpoints to our app, followed by good old-fashioned `print` statements.

Understanding breakpoints

Breakpoints have been around for a while now, and not just in Xcode – other IDEs such as Visual Studio make great use of breakpoints to debug applications on the fly.

In a nutshell, by adding a breakpoint at a specific line in your code, when running the app from the IDE, should the line of code where you have placed the breakpoint be hit, the code will pause at this point and allow you inspect any variable that might be available at that time.

The following is an example of a breakpoint in Xcode. A currently active breakpoint will appear in light blue, as shown here:

```
14
15      static func saveRecipes(recipes: [RecipeModel]) {
16          let data = try! JSONEncoder().encode(recipes)
17          UserDefaults.standard.set(data, forKey: "recipes")
18      }
```

If you single-click the breakpoint, it will turn gray and become inactive. Xcode will then move past this, should it get called. To remove the breakpoint completely, single-click and hold the breakpoint and then drag it away.

Let's take a look at what a breakpoint looks like when our debugger is paused on that particular line:

```
15          static func saveRecipes(recipes: [RecipeModel]) {
16              let data = try! JSONEncoder().encode(recipes)                    ⊟  Thread 1: breakpoint 2.1
17              UserDefaults.standard.set(data, forKey: "recipes")
```

At this moment, all activity in your app will have stopped and you'll be able to inspect any variable that is currently in scope. Let's take a look at the recipe variable being passed into our saveRecipes() functions.

Inspecting variables

If you hover over recipes and expand the current collection, you'll be able to see the array of RecipeModel() currently being passed in:

```
tic func saveRecipes(recipes: [RecipeModel]) {

    ▼ 8 values
U       ▶ [0] (My_Favourite_Recipes.RecipeModel)                        e
        ▶ [1] (My_Favourite_Recipes.RecipeModel)
        ▶ [2] (My_Favourite_Recipes.RecipeModel)
Ge      ▶ [3] (My_Favourite_Recipes.RecipeModel)
ti      ▶ [4] (My_Favourite_Recipes.RecipeModel)       ⊙ ⓘ              c
        ▶ [5] (My_Favourite_Recipes.RecipeModel)
i       ▶ [6] (My_Favourite_Recipes.RecipeModel)                       y
                                                                       i
```

Another place we can see the variables is in the **Watch Window** situated at the bottom of Xcode. Again, both functions and class variables will be shown here, along with the option to evaluate them:

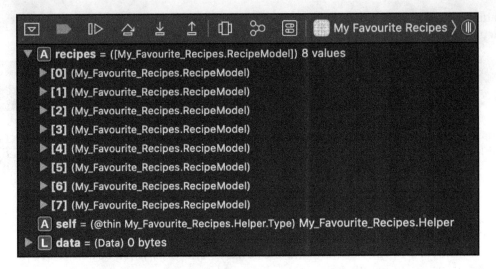

This is a great way to quickly see what values are stored in our variable at a particular moment in our code. However, we can be a little more interactive with the console window.

Understanding the console window

To the right of the Watch Window is the console. When your app is running, Xcode will automatically output any data that's been pushed to the console here. However, when you hit a breakpoint, you can input commands to check the value of a variable, condition, or even a function for yourself. Let's take a look at how we would do this:

```
(lldb) po recipes
▼ 8 elements
  ▼ 0 : RecipeModel
    - id : 6A21FB42-9BFB-443F-B053-301C2FCA8D83
    - name : "Chips"
    - origin : "Italy"
    - countryCode : ""
    - favourite : false
    ▼ ingredients : 1 element
      - 0 : "Potato"
    - recipe : "Slice and dice"
    - imageData : nil
  ▼ 1 : RecipeModel
    - id : 94CAEE8E-5ABA-4917-8A2F-E6A515DC652D
    - name : "Jnklml"
    - origin : "Italy"
    - countryCode : ""
    - favourite : false
    - ingredients : 0 elements
    - recipe : ""
    - imageData : nil
  ▼ 2 : RecipeModel
    - id : 98E47DFB-1BF3-472A-9865-121F812C9D74
    - name : "Frehy"
    - origin : "Italy"
```

With us still held at our breakpoint, you'll notice that we've typed in po recipes (*'po'* *stands for 'print object'*). the print object basically prints the result value of the object or function straight to the console window.

Another option would be to use dump(). Working in a similar way to print, dump will output the full class hierarchy for more complex objects (for example, if you have objects within objects), thus making a little easier for us to deep dive into the world of debugging. If you are seeing a model and its children for the first time, dump() would be a great way to get to know the workings of this.

To perform a dump, just type the following:

```
(lldb) po dump(recipes)
```

You'll still need to perform a *print object* in order to put the result on the screen.

This is a great way to check for variables when they're held at a breakpoint, but you may want to check multiple values in quick succession, and constantly being stopped by a breakpoint is not ideal.

This is where the `print()` statement comes into the picture. Back in Xcode, we can use the `print()` statement in our code in order to output the value of variables straight to the console, all while our app is running. Let's take a look at how we'd do that:

```
// Update Local Saved Data
self.appData.recipes.append(newRecipe)
Helper.saveRecipes(recipes: self.appData.recipes)
WatchManager.sharedInstance.send(recipe: newRecipe)
print(newRecipe)
```

Here, in `AddRecipeView.swift`, we've added a `print` statement for our `newRecipe` that's being saved. When our code is run and this function is hit, the `print` statement will output directly to the console.

We can be a bit creative with our `print` statements too. Here, we've prefixed our printed object with some text so that we can easily identify this in our console:

```
print("New Recipe: \(newRecipe)")
```

We can also make use of the `dump()` command:

```
print(dump(newRecipe))
```

The console window can offer so much more than we need to cover in this book, from filtering the outputted text to running functions. These basics will certainly help you get off the ground and make you feel more comfortable with debugging in Xcode.

Other tools to consider

Xcode really is bursting with features to be proud of and a lot of them are out of the scope of this book. However, I couldn't leave this chapter without mentioning a couple of things to take note of, should you fancy dipping your toes further into the water.

Instruments

Instruments has been around in Xcode since the early days. With each release growing stronger and more powerful, it's become a must-have for any iOS developer.

Packed with features such as Time Profiler and System Tracing and with the ability to detect memory leaks, it's a must-have tool, especially if you are planning on deploying a large-scale application:

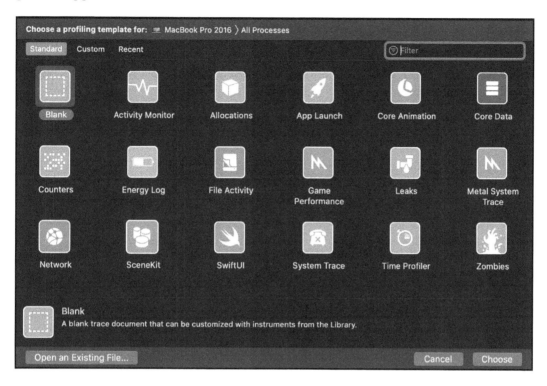

Instruments can be found via Xcode by clicking on **Xcode | Open Developer Tool | Instruments**.

Analyze

Analyze is a static analyzer built directly into Xcode. These days, static analysis plays a big part in many types of development projects. Analyze, as a tool, can offer the following in terms of features for your current project:

- Logic flaws and uninitialized variables
- Memory leaks and bad management
- Suggestions on API usages that don't conform to Apple's Framework guidelines

Analyze can be found from Xcode's menu bar by clicking on **Product | Analyze**.

Summary

In this chapter, we've covered how to start testing with UI Testing and Unit Testing. We do this by creating new targets in our current project and learning the fundamental basics of how to write the tests. We also looked at the differences between them and why they coexist in Xcode.

Then, we looked at debugging and explored the most common tools used for debugging, such as breakpoints, the Watch Window, and the output console.

We wrapped up the section by looking at some of the other tools that are available that you may wish to explore.

The only thing left to do is grab that second coffee and give yourself a big pat on the back - with everything we've covered during the course of this book - you'll have no trouble getting up and running building your first SwiftUI project - good luck and thank you for coming along for the ride!

Questions

1. What are the two fundamental differences between UI and Unit Tests?
2. How do we add a UI or Unit Test to our current project?
3. How should we word the name of the function for a test?
4. What is the name of Xcode's test suite?
5. How would we output a class hierarchy to the console window?

Further reading

- **MobileA11y Blog:** https://mobilea11y.com/
- **Static Analyzer:** https://developer.apple.com/library/archive/documentation/DeveloperTools/Conceptual/debugging_with_xcode/chapters/static_analyzer.html

Other Books You May Enjoy

If you enjoyed this book, you may be interested in these other books by Packt:

iOS 13 Programming for Beginners - Fourth Edition
Ahmad Sahar, Craig Clayton

ISBN: 978-1-83882-190-6

- Get to grips with the fundamentals of Xcode 11 and Swift 5, the building blocks of iOS development
- Understand how to prototype an app using storyboards
- Discover the Model-View-Controller design pattern, and how to implement the desired functionality within the app
- Implement the latest iOS features such as Dark Mode and Sign In with Apple
- Understand how to convert an existing iPad app into a Mac app
- Design, deploy, and test your iOS applications with industry patterns and practices

Mastering Swift 5 - Fifth Edition
Jon Hoffman

ISBN: 978-1-78913-986-0

- Understand core Swift components, including operators, collections, control flows, and functions
- Learn how and when to use classes, structures, and enumerations
- Understand how to use protocol-oriented design with extensions to write easier-to-manage code
- Use design patterns with Swift, to solve commonly occurring design problems
- Implement copy-on-write for you custom value types to improve performance
- Add concurrency to your applications using Grand Central Dispatch and Operation Queues
- Implement generics to write flexible and reusable code

Leave a review - let other readers know what you think

Please share your thoughts on this book with others by leaving a review on the site that you bought it from. If you purchased the book from Amazon, please leave us an honest review on this book's Amazon page. This is vital so that other potential readers can see and use your unbiased opinion to make purchasing decisions, we can understand what our customers think about our products, and our authors can see your feedback on the title that they have worked with Packt to create. It will only take a few minutes of your time, but is valuable to other potential customers, our authors, and Packt. Thank you!

Index

www.ingramcontent.com/pod-product-compliance
Lightning Source LLC
Chambersburg PA
CBHW080625060326
40690CB00021B/4819